Cleveland Summertime Memories

A WARM LOOK BACK

Gail Ghetia Bellamy

GRAY & COMPANY, PUBLISHERS
CLEVELAND

To my husband, Stephen Paul Bellamy

Gray & Company, Publishers
www.grayco.com

Designed by Laurence J. Nozik

Library of Congress Cataloging-in-Publication Data
Bellamy, Gail.
Cleveland summertime memories / Gail Ghetia Bellamy.
pages cm
Includes bibliographical references and index.
ISBN 978-1-938441-50-9 (alk. paper)

1. Bellamy, Gail--Childhood and youth. 2. Cleveland (Ohio)--Social life and customs--20th century. 3. Summer--Ohio--Cleveland--History--20th century. I. Title.

F499.C65B45 2013
977.1'32--dc23
2013038063

ISBN: 978-1-938441-50-9

Printed in the United States of America
1

CONTENTS

WHAT'S YOUR PLEASURE? Swimming, fishing, amusement parks, drive-in movies, ice cream stands, miniature golf . . . put them all together, and it's summer.

INTRODUCTION

Is it Summer Yet?

Whether it's summer in Cleveland depends on how you define the season. Some say local summers start with the opening day of the Cleveland Indians baseball season, Memorial Day, the day the gates are thrown open at community swimming pools, the day your boat goes in the water, or the day the concession stands open at your favorite beach. Does it end the day after Labor Day, or when the calendar tells us it's September 21? Maybe summer hangs on until you finally put the porch furniture away in October or November.

For kids, the summer might be defined differently. It starts on the last day of school, the first day of softball, or at the first sighting of the neighborhood ice cream truck. It ends when the fall school term starts and the last Popsicle is eaten on the front porch.

When it comes to summer memories, one thing is sure: It's not numbers that tell the story—how many people showed up at Municipal Stadium during an Indians season, or how many swimming pools were open in the City of Cleveland in a particular year. It's people who share their memories of summer and make yesteryear come alive.

In case you think summer is the same in every city, think again. We live on the shores of Lake Erie, dwell in the vortex of roller coaster heaven, enjoy Major League Baseball, listen to outdoor summer music played by the Cleveland Orchestra—one of the greatest orchestras in the world—and immerse ourselves in rock concerts and picnics that honor nationalities in the home of the Rock and Roll Hall of Fame and the National Cleveland-Style Polka Hall of Fame.

When you were a kid here, didn't it seem that summer sped by? Perhaps that was the influence of events like the Cleveland National Air Races, the summer schedule at area racetracks and speedways, and the rides at kiddie parks and amusement parks. Once a year on the Fourth of July we slowed down to appreciate fireworks at Edgewater Park, watching as bursts of color and the moon reflected off one of the largest bodies of fresh water in the world.

You know you're a Clevelander if your summertime memories involve seeing Jungle Larry not only on the *Captain Penny* television show but also in person at Puritas Springs Park, Chippewa Lake, or Cedar Point. You watched the Ghoulardi All-Stars play ball or drank a Big Ghoulardi cool shake at your neighborhood Manners Restaurant. You attended concerts and saw big-name bands during the World Series of Rock at the Cleveland Municipal Stadium, cruised on Lake Erie aboard the Aquarama, went all the way downtown for a Frosty Malt in Higbee's basement, ordered too many hot dogs at the ballgame because you loved the mustard, and waited all year to have a Frozen Whip or Humphrey's Candy Kisses at Euclid Beach Park. You'll experience an even bigger taste of summers past on the pages that follow.

AVOID BELLY FLOPS; NO CANNONBALLS ALLOWED:
Learning to swim was a rite of summer in the '60s.

COOL IT!

BEACHES, POOLS, AND OTHER COOL PLACES

Staying cool, Cleveland-style, meant taking advantage of nearby beaches and swimming pools. Lake Erie is the 12th-largest lake in the world in surface area, and we enjoy its 871 miles of shoreline and 9,910 square miles of water surface area (4,977 miles of it in the U.S.). That's a lot of territory to splash around in. Then, think of the more than 40 local public swimming pools in the City of Cleveland alone. Add to that the number of suburban swimming pools, smaller lakes, and rivers in the region. No wonder we've created so many swimming, boating, and beach memories over the years.

Beach Memories

Cleveland-area residents packed up their coolers and swimsuits and headed to the lakefront. While many stayed close to home at Edgewater Park, Huntington Beach, Gordon Park, and Mentor Headlands, others headed farther east or west. They succumbed to the siren song of places like the Strip along Lake Road in Geneva-on-the-Lake and attractions like Allison's, the country's oldest continuously operating miniature golf course, which has been open since 1924. Other spots included Lakeview Park in Lorain with its iconic concrete Easter basket filled with flowers, and Port Clinton, Catawba Island, Lakeside, and other areas where city folks could enjoy the leisurely pace of summers along the Lake Erie shoreline. Many of these memories involve sunburns.

**THE NUMBERS:
CLEVELAND INDIANS
HOME ATTENDANCE**

1950: 1,727,464

1960: 950,985

1970: 729,752

1980: 1,033,827

1990: 1,225,240

2000: 3,456,278

THE NUMBERS: LAKE ERIE

Length in miles: 241

Miles of shoreline: 871

Commercial fish yield in the 1950s: 75 million pounds

**THE NUMBERS:
AMUSEMENT PARKS**

Back in the early 1900s, Ohio was home to 54 amusement parks.

LAKE VIEW:
Lakeview Park in Lorain.

MENTOR HEADLANDS

When school let out for summer vacation, I could think of only one thing: going to Lake Erie. I remember the 45-minute drive from my home in Cleveland Heights out to Mentor Headlands always seemed so long—the anticipation of going to the beach almost too much for my 5-year-old self to bear. When we'd finally arrive, the scads of cars in the parking lot announced the crowds that swarmed the beach, making the blood race through my veins, urging my little body to sprint out onto the sand and claim a spot as fast as possible. As quickly as I'd choose a post for my towel and toys, I would abandon it for the lapping shore. As a small girl, the expanse of Lake Erie often made me feel that I was at the ocean. My favorite thing to do once in the water was to lie on my back in the wet sand with my feet pointed out at the horizon, letting the waves rush over my body and swish me to and fro. From this angle, those waves looked giant as they rolled in and curled over me. I remember feeling so small but so full of joy as my Great Lake welcomed me into summer. —*Stephanie Gautam*

GORDON PARK, 1913:
A site for summer fun in Cleveland.

BEACHES AT CEDAR POINT, MARBLEHEAD, GEM BEACH, CATAWBA, AND BAY POINT

My childhood summertime memories revolve around Lake Erie. While growing up in a large family, we didn't venture too far from home. Fortunately for us, Lake Erie provided enough fun and entertainment for the whole family. Our favorite one-tank trip was west to Cedar Point.

My dad worked for an insurance company and his client was Cedar Point. All of us accompanied him each time he made the trip to the park, which seemed to be often.

Back then, Cedar Point did not charge a gate fee. It was free to get in and you only paid for each individual ride. The big attraction for us back then was not the rides, it was the beach, where we spent all day.

Besides our trips to Cedar Point, my parents rented cabins at Marblehead, Gem Beach, Catawba, and Bay Point. During our stay in Marblehead, we also visited African Lion Safari (which I was not a fan of). I never understood the concept of allowing people to drive through an area with giraffes sticking their heads through open car windows and water buffalo pressing their faces up against your car to get food.

LIFE IN 1964:
A view of Mentor Headlands.

Other "fun" adventures were to Mystery Hill, the Blue Hole, Lagoon Deer Park, and South Bass Island.

As adults, we are now making frequent trips to the dermatologist, since sunscreen did not become available until after our childhood beach adventures. —*Lynne McLaughlin*

LINWOOD PARK IN VERMILION

We used to go to Linwood Park, in Vermilion next to the lagoon, in the early '60s. There were cottages and a really old amusement park, Crystal Beach, next to it. I remember being able to shoot a .22 there. The rifles were chained up and you could shoot at targets. The rifles weren't very accurate. We used to rent the same cottage every year, a few houses from the beach. I remember getting sunburned. —*Dave Davis*

ROCKY RIVER BEACH

My favorite place was Lake Erie. I can remember when we were young and would go out, my mom would say, "Stay away from the lake." The first place you would go was the lake. Before the famous storm on July 4th, 1969, the beaches were really nice. We could walk all the way from Rocky River Park to Pier 9 on the beach. After that storm, the beaches were wiped out. —*Noreen Hone*

LIVING ALONG THE LAKE

I lived on Kensington Oval in Rocky River. We were almost on the water; we weren't on the beach, it was up on a cliff. We had one of those jalousie porches, and in the morning you'd find my mother out there, just watching the lake because we were so close. We could walk down to the beach from our house. In those days, in the 1960s, you couldn't go in the water.

THE BUCK STOPS HERE: Lagoon Deer Park, Sandusky in the 1970s.

GOTTA GET TO THE REGATTA: In this case, the 1992 Horseshoe Lake Regatta in Shaker Heights.

BEER HERE: Candy bars and beverages were offered at the Gordon Park concession stand, August 1938.

They really hadn't cleaned up the lake or the river at that point. There were lifeguards posted there to keep you out of the water, not to guard you while you were in the water. So we would go down there, but we had to stay on the beach. I remember one time I had skinned my knee, and we somehow were able to walk in the water. My mother found out, and within a minute I was soaking my knee in Epsom salts because she had a total fit to think that I had an open wound and had gotten Lake Erie water on it.

It was really lovely to have the lake there, and see all the moods the lake could bring to the seasons. In the summer, I remember looking out at the lake from our open windows. You could hear it. —*Maribeth Katt*

GENEVA-ON-THE-LAKE

It was the oldest summer resort. I went there in the 1960s, and then I went there with my son in the 1970s. A friend of mine owned cottages there.
—*George Popovich*

EAST HARBOR

I'm the youngest of seven kids. At least once a year we went up to East Harbor. When we went there, it was a little like approaching Cedar Point. You know, you'd drive for an hour and then start seeing the lake and you'd think you were close. But then you'd keep driving and driving and driving. Since you're a little kid, it seems like it's another three hours before you get there. Eventually, you get to the parking lot, and that goes on forever. You park, and the lake is on the other side of a little dune. It's like, "There it is! Wow!" We went up for only a day. We never stayed overnight. We'd go in the water, sit on the blankets and harass each other.
—*Joe Gunderman*

PORT CLINTON

For years our family vacation was at the National Rifle Matches at Camp Perry. —*Lynette Macias*

GEAUGA LAKE

My great-uncle and his brothers built a cottage in the 1930s and 1940s on a piece of property opposite Geauga Lake. Every summer in the 1950s, the family went out there and spent the summer at this cottage. It was on the other side of the lake, back from where SeaWorld eventually was. Residents had access to a swimming area in the lake. Normally

A SIGN OF SUMMER:
Swimming at
Edgewater Beach.

CAMPERS AT PORT CLINTON:
Just one of many places to
enjoy the summer sun.

swimming was not allowed for the public, but there was a small section to the right of the park with a dock, a diving board, a raft, and everything. We were able to get a pass every summer so we swam and rafted there, and then we enjoyed the park in the evening. —*Dennis Gaughan*

Signs of the Unofficial Start of Summer

In Cleveland, we don't like to restrict ourselves to calendar dates roping off the confines of summer from June 21 until September 21. Some say summer starts with Memorial Day and ends the day after Labor Day. Others define summer as the weeks when local schools aren't in session or the weeks when area swimming pools have water in them. For instance, the City of Cleveland pools open in mid-May, with a season that runs through Labor Day. Chowhounds consider the dates when seasonal ice cream stands are open for business. Meanwhile, here are a few more ideas about what marks the official start of summer in Cleveland.

SUMMER = BASEBALL; BASEBALL = SUMMER

I now know that summer begins in April with the home opener, and ends only when the last game of the World Series is over, but when I was a kid, I couldn't have cared less about baseball. My father and my two older brothers were serious baseball fans. They spent most of the summer in our third-floor TV room watching baseball. I'd pass through every once in a while and ask them why they were yelling, and which uniforms our team was wearing—the black or the white ones (we did not have a color TV). I'd watch for a few minutes, then get bored, and wander down to the kitchen for an orange Popsicle or a glass of iced tea. But I loved the baseball sounds that followed me down the stairs. The relaxed, unaccented play-by-play: "high and outside," "line drive," "pop fly to center field." Sheer poetry. —*Meredith Holmes*

SCHOOL'S OUT FOR SUMMER

The first "official" sign of summer is not the weather getting nice. Being married to a schoolteacher and having boys, I think of the last day of school as the beginning of summer. After getting through the weekend, on that first Monday, summer is here. That, and going to the Rec Center in Chagrin Falls. We would pack our lunch, go early in the morning for swimming lessons, and stay all day. —*Nancy Hudson Snell*

HIGH POINT OF THE SUMMER: Swimming at beaches such as Edgewater Park was a timeless way to keep cool.

WAY OUT WEST: The Hotel Westlake, Rocky River, was built in 1925. Celebrities such as Charles Lindbergh and Amelia Earhart were among its guests when it was the National Air Races headquarters hotel.

Summer Swimming Hijinks

Sometimes, parents were better off not knowing about the summertime memories their kids were creating.

CLIFTON BEACH IN LAKEWOOD

We used to dive off the top railing of the lighthouse there. It had to be at least four or five stories. You'd get on the top railing and wait for waves to come in. The water was only about 12 feet deep, and when a high wave came, you had to dive out to miss the big rocks at the bottom. I can't even believe I did that. Somebody dared me. The only reason I could do it was that I went to Wildwood Quarries and I used to dive off the rocks there. I got used to going higher and higher. It was pretty stupid, but I didn't get hurt. One time I actually dove into a big fish—a carp or something—under the water.

Another thing we did was swim up to a floating log or tree. We used it like a float that we could paddle on, and we'd see how far we could go. We would go across the mouth of Rocky River and try to go to Wildwood. We'd get pretty far, and then turn around.

—*Steve Horniak*

THE SOUND OF THE BELL

When warm weather hit, I considered it summer-like, but the first day of summer was when we walked out of the school after the last bell rang. Summer had officially started. It was an epiphany-type moment. The clouds opened up, the sun came out and shone on me. It was a religious moment.
—*Steve Presser*

READING INTO IT

Summer kick-off always meant going to the Arlington Library (Cleveland Public Library Branch) to sign up for the Summer Reading Club. I loved to read, and still do. You got to attend a special party at the end of summer if you read 10 or more books. That was a snap, but if you read more they wouldn't count any more than the initial 10. —*Donna "Dahmia" Komidar*

SINGING INTO SUMMER

The beginning of summer is the first day you hear John Fogerty singing "Centerfield" (Put me in, Coach). —*Pat Fernberg*

PRACTICING FOR SUMMER

When I was a real little kid, the beginning of summer probably meant starting baseball practice, which was in May. They were kind of cold Saturday mornings. I played in Middleburg Heights, in the City League.
—*Joe Gunderman*

A SWINGING GOOD TIME ON JULY FOURTH: Edgewater Park was the place to be, 1980.

WHAT A DIVE: Enjoying a swim at the new Bretton Ridge pool in North Olmsted, 1965.

Cool Pools

Ah, the smell of chlorine, the toe checks for athlete's foot at community pools, the rules that had girls wearing bathing caps, and always having to wait an hour after eating before you went in swimming.

SHAW POOL

I have great memories of going to Shaw Pool as a kid growing up on the border of Cleveland and East Cleveland. I took free swimming lessons there in the 1950s. During the 1960s, a group of us gals would go to the upper deck of Shaw Pool for the dances that were held there every week during the summer. Ladies' Choice was always a particular favorite, when you could summon the courage to ask that boy to dance, since he hadn't the nerve to walk all the way across the expanse of deck away from his buddies.

—Donna "Dahmia" Komidar

SWIMMING IN BEREA

I always swam in the pool rather than the quarries because I wanted to be able to see in the water—to see the kids, and be safe. For 45 years, I have been a water safety instructor, mostly in Berea. One year we had a phantom pooper in the kiddie pool. We had to drain it and clean it. We never knew if it was a person or some animal, maybe a raccoon. —Joann Rae Macias

(continued)

WILDWOOD LAKE ON COLUMBIA ROAD

As a teenager in the late '60s I remember going to Wildwood Park with my friends for a day of sunning (I should say sunburning) and swimming. I remember the admission was like $1, and my friends figured out a way to sneak in by tramping through the surrounding woods. We would be all scratched up by the time we managed to get in.

—Peggy King-Neumann

NO HELMET, NO HANDS, NO SUNSCREEN

Daily we would make the three-mile trek by bike to Cumberland Pool in Cleveland Heights. Swimming all day (with no SPF) was the norm. Heading back home, we would ride through the back streets, with no helmets and no hands, so that our dad wouldn't catch us riding in the streets.

—Sally Slater Wilson

HANDS DOWN: Community pools such as Cumberland in Cleveland Heights made summers sweeter.

READY, SET, GO!: Back in 1963, girls were required to wear bathing caps at swimming pools, including the Mentor Yacht Club Pool.

"It was cool to find a quarry or a stream to splash around in."

SWIMMING IN LAKEWOOD

We spent afternoons swimming at Lakewood Pool. We walked from Bonnieview Avenue to Summit Avenue for summer school, then walked home for lunch. After lunch, we rode our bikes to the park. We sat on benches in the hot sun waiting to be let in. Admission was 10 cents, a small price for my mother to pay for some peace and quiet and possibly a nap. —*Helen Wirt*

SEARCHING FOR CUMBERLAND POOL (IT'S IN CLEVELAND HEIGHTS)

The first summer I lived in Cleveland Heights, it took me a while to get to Cumberland, the city's public, outdoor pool. There were two reasons for this. First, it's hard to find because it's completely camouflaged, hidden behind trees and big bushes. Second, none of my friends would go swimming with me. They didn't own bathing suits, only cut-off jeans. Some of them had beards, and they all had long hair. This was 1974, the twilight of the Age of Aquarius. It wasn't cool to swim at a nice, clean municipal pool. It was cool to find a quarry or a stream to splash around in. If you had a car, which I did not, you might go, once a summer, to Punderson State Park. Not good enough. I wanted to swim every day, so I ditched the peer pressure. I dug out my bathing suit, scraped together the money for a season swimming pass, and rode my yellow Huffy to Cumberland Pool. I jumped into that beautiful, chlorinated water in June and stayed until the end of August. Heaven! —*Meredith Holmes*

AVON LAKE POOL

You were living large if you had a summer pass to the Avon Lake pool and somehow hung out at Huntington Park in Bay Village prior to getting a driver's license. —*Paul Negulescu*

OUT TO LAUNCH: June 1976, the boat launch in Rocky River Reservation Scenic Park offered a way to start the day on Lake Erie.

Enjoying the Water

Boating and fishing have long been favorite summer activities in Cleveland. According to the Ohio Department of Natural Resources, Division of Watercraft, Cuyahoga County claimed 24,800 boat registrations in 2012. In fact, 3.1 million of the state's 11.5 million residents live within 10 miles of either Lake Erie or the Ohio River.

In decades past, as today, some folks sailed to enjoy the lake, the sun, and the scenery. Others were competitors, or avid fishers, enjoying the bounty of regional waters. In the 1950s, Lake Erie yielded 75 million pounds of commercial fish. In 1968, more than a dozen eligible fish species were listed in The Second Annual Sun Newspapers Big Fish Contest. Fish species included largemouth and smallmouth bass, white bass, rock bass, crappie, carp, perch, walleye, northern pike, rainbow trout, channel catfish, bluegill, muskellunge, bullhead, sheepshead, and smelt.

SAILING INTO SUMMER

When my husband and I were first married, we connected with two families who owned sailboats, and they asked us to crew at Edgewater for the races. We had a wonderful time sailing the races at Edgewater. The sailboat was a J/30. —*Nancy Hudson Snell*

BOATING FROM CHAGRIN YACHT CLUB TO PUT-IN-BAY AND CEDAR POINT

Arriving at the harbor at Put-in-Bay on South Bass Island after a six-hour boat ride, we could hardly wait to walk from the docks to Frosty's to have a frosted mug of cold root beer. Our dad was equally eager for the infamous Frosty beer! We would crunch through the peanut shells on the floor to play our favorite tunes on the jukebox while waiting for our pizza. Afterward, we

RELAXING DAY OF FISHING: Tranquility was the word at Gordon Park, 1962.

ARRIVING IN STYLE: Boaters at Cedar Point docks.

Local High-Profile Boats

Not everybody who lived on Lake Erie owned a boat or even knew somebody who did, but locals seized opportunities to experience Lake Erie and the Cuyahoga River in style.

THE S.S. AQUARAMA

When the Aquarama passenger ship made its inaugural voyage between Cleveland's West 3rd Street Pier and the city of Detroit in 1957, it was the largest passenger ship on the Great Lakes. The trip took six hours. Converted from a World War II troop ship, the 520-foot-long Aquarama accommodated 2,500 passengers and claimed a top cruising speed of more than 22 miles an hour. With a futuristic design, the ship's many "firsts" included elevators and closed-circuit television enabling observation from the pilot house. Every deck offered entertainment pleasures for passengers aboard the ship. For instance, the Upper Deck included a candy, cigarette, and souvenir counter; cocktail lounges and bars; soda and sandwich bar; main stage and dancing. Then there was the Club Deck, which had a TV room, a children's playroom, and more dancing and food places. The Sports Deck featured an observation lounge and observation deck, and finally, there was the Sun Deck. The Aquarama's last voyage took place the day after Labor Day 1962.

would play in DeRivera Park on the cannon (the war memorial from the Battle of Lake Erie). We would then cruise over to Cedar Point amusement park, stay overnight on the boat, and spend the next day riding rides and eating potato fries with vinegar. —*Sally Slater Wilson*

VACATIONS ON THE LAKE: The Put-in-Bay Ferry, Perry's Victory and International Peace Memorial at Put-in-Bay, and the 1960s Beachcomber Motor Lodge overlooking the lake on West Erie Avenue in Lorain.

SEA SNARK

We weren't big boaters, but at one point, my dad got himself a Styrofoam Sea Snark sailboat from Sears. It was one of those triangular sail jobs that you can rig in about a minute. He decided to put some fiberglass on the bottom of it. My dad's very handy, but let's put it this way: There were a lot of bubbles in that fiberglass. We'd take it out and fumble our way across sailing. Just about the time he got that boat, I ran into a friend whose family was all about sailing. They had a 27-foot boat out at Lakeside Yacht Club. So very shortly after my dad got his little Sea Snark, I was actually sailing with my friend as his crew. I don't know that much about it, but if you tell me to pull that rope, I can pull it. —*Joe Gunderman*

STEALTH FISHING

I got my first fishing rod when I was five, and 52 years later I still have it—not for fishing, but for the glorious memories it holds. On Saturdays, my dad and I got up early and headed to the diner in Lakewood for breakfast. We always ordered the same thing—cheeseburgers, sardines, and Cokes. My dad made this ritual seem as if it were a sneaky adventure, saying, "For God's sake, don't tell your mother I let you eat sardines and a cheeseburger for breakfast." After our "forbidden" breakfast, we'd drive down the hill into the valley (Rocky River Reservation) and head straight

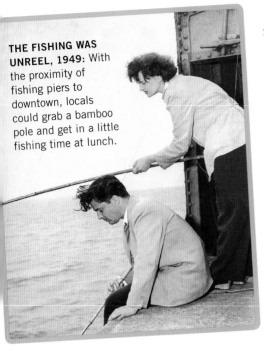

THE FISHING WAS UNREEL, 1949: With the proximity of fishing piers to downtown, locals could grab a bamboo pole and get in a little fishing time at lunch.

for the wall at Eddie's Boat Dock. We'd sit on the wall and fish for a few hours. My dad would warn me, "Don't tell your mother I let you sit on the wall with your feet hanging over!" The feeling that we were being sneaky was half the fun. It took several years for me to catch on that my parents didn't keep secrets from each other, and these Saturday morning escapades were not a sneaky secret between my dad and me.

—Laurie Ghetia-Orr

SUMMER JOB

In the summer of 1977, my family had just moved back to Cleveland after living in Florida since my sister and I were very young. My parents took my sister Nancy, who was 11, and me (I was 14) on a trip downtown to do some sight-seeing. One of the places we went to was the Soldiers' and Sailors' Monument on Public Square. We were able to see my grandfather's name inscribed on the wall because he had served in World War I.

Toward the end of the day, we were walking down by the East 9th Street pier. Seems to me that we were going to get something to eat at Captain Frank's. That is when I saw her. She was the most beautiful thing that I had seen in my 14 years on this planet. I couldn't take my eyes off her. I asked my parents if we could walk over so I could see her better. They obliged.

I remember back then she was all gray, and she was only 34 years old. There was an older gentleman standing by a gate. "Welcome aboard!" he said. "Do you want to take a tour?"

I turned to my parents, ready to beg, but my Dad answered quickly: "Sure!" The older man showed us through the gate. "This is the submarine U.S.S. *Cod*. I am Doggie Dishong, and I served on her for the last five of her seven war patrols during World War II."

He showed us the proper way to board a boat. We walked through the Cod, listening to Doggie's stories. I hung on Doggie's every word, and asked a lot of questions. It was the best almost-two-hours that I had ever spent in my life! On our way home, I made up my mind that I wanted to be a submarine sailor, like Doggie Dishong, and ride on a submarine like the Cod. This was all I could think about as I got ready for bed. The next morning, I was up early. I asked my parents if I could take the 39 bus downtown and

(continued)

THE GOODTIME

In the late 1950s, the Goodtime offered Lake Erie harbor and Cuyahoga River tours on a boat that accommodated 68 people. In 1962, the larger Goodtime II arrived on the scene. It had a capacity of 475 people for river tours on the Cuyahoga. The Goodtime II sailed six miles along the Cuyahoga River, passing under 21 bridges. Today, the tradition continues. The Goodtime III excursion ship accommodates 1,000 passengers.

THE U.S.S. COD

The U.S.S. Cod Submarine Memorial, a World War II fleet submarine, was designated a National Historic Landmark in 1986. The U.S.S. Cod's permanent location is on Lake Erie in downtown Cleveland, adjacent to Burke Lakefront Airport. Tours have been available since 1976.

You Know What Else Was Cool? Trendy Summer Fashions!

MADRAS ON WHEELS

Until 7th grade, I had no concept of fashion. Then I noticed people were wearing white Levis. By the end of 7th grade, madras came out. Then, if you were really cool, you got bleeding madras. That was when skateboards first hit, too. If you had a skateboard and bleeding madras, you were the ultimate in cool. After 1964, when the Beatles hit, nobody wanted a flattop or crewcut haircut. We also wore loafers with no socks—because surfers didn't wear socks—and nobody wore white socks because Ghoulardi made fun of them.

—*Dave Davis*

CLAMDIGGERS

I have a picture of myself wearing clamdiggers with a rope belt.

—*Larry Fox*

DANCING IN THE STREETS

I loved to dress up as a hula dancer. In 1962, I insisted that I was going to walk in the Lakewood Day Parade, wearing my grass skirt and a lei. The parade always included kids who decorated their bikes with crepe paper and streamers. I just entered the parade in the middle, and my dad walked along the sidelines while I danced the hula until I was exhausted. Half the fun was being allowed to be in the middle of the

go see the Cod again. They gave me the okay, and I ate some breakfast and was out the door.

If memory serves, it was 8:30 when I got down to the boat. I saw the sign saying that she did not open until 10, so I waited as patiently as I could. When Doggie arrived, about 9:30, he remembered me immediately. He asked me if I would go aboard with him and help him open up the boat, which I did gladly. I spent the entire day there and caught the 39 bus home at 5 p.m. I went back every day for the next week, and walked through the boat with Doggie, listening to his stories and the stories of the other submarine veterans.

The following week, I again showed up early to help Doggie open up the boat. This time, the tours he was giving were a little different. He began asking me questions during the tours. I answered them eagerly in front of the captive audiences. At the end of the day, I was doing a final walk-through with him, closing up the boat for the night. As we parted, he said rather flatly, "I suppose you are going to be here tomorrow."

"Yes!" I answered excitedly, "I love this boat!"

"As do I," Doggie replied. "Be here early, because you are going to be working for me. You are going to be giving tours and helping me keep the old girl in shipshape."

I was so excited, you can't imagine! This was my first job, and he even wanted to pay me! Needless to say, I worked on the Cod every summer, and on the weekends when I was in school and she was open. When I was 16, I begged my parents to let me join the Navy. They allowed me to join the Delayed Entry Program, and I was guaranteed submarines. I spent 10 years riding submarines, loving every minute of it

Doggie passed away in 1983, but he was able to see that I had earned my "Dolphins." He was so proud. I think of him often, and go down to the Cod every chance I get. —*Mark Rhoades*

HISTORY NOTE: The U.S.S. Cod was launched in March, 1943 and made seven World War II patrol runs.

CATCH OF THE DAY: Fishers explored the bounty of regional waters.

SUMMER STRATEGY: Making the most of a summer day at Edgewater Park, 1975.

(continued)

street, which normally was forbidden territory meant only for traffic. If you were riding a bike in the parade, you couldn't catch candy being thrown from the floats. My rogue hula exhibition was short-lived due to exhaustion, but I got the most candy that year as a bonus.

—*Laurie Ghetia-Orr*

A SHOE-IN FOR SUMMER

We hit summertime hard. Most of the guys felt the same way. For summertime, you got your special shoes. For us, the shoe of choice back then was the low Jack Purcell, in white. And it was great to indoctrinate the shoes. When someone got a pair of shoes, they were white for about 9/10 of a second. You would step on them. You couldn't do it to yourself; you couldn't dirty up your own shoes. Your buddies had to get you into the club. You'd come home and your mother would say, "What did you do to your shoes?" We'd say, "I was out playing. I was out with the guys." You know, every kid had the same answer.

Very few kids in my neighborhood wore Speedos to go swimming. We frowned upon guys who wore Speedos. For us, it was cut-off shorts. I remember cutting the shorts and fraying the bottom. There was an art form to it.

—*Steve Presser*

QUITE A SPREAD: A picnic on newspaper-covered tables at Squire's Castle, 1953, in North Chagrin Reservation.

GET OUT!

The Great Outdoors, From Parks to Playgrounds

The Cleveland Metroparks make up the state's oldest park district. Since 1917 we've reveled in its acres of parkland. By 1939, the Metroparks included 60 miles of bridle paths, 55 miles of road, 53 miles of hiking trails and 33 picnic grounds. By July 1951, as many as 7,000 people flocked to Wallace Lake to cool off. Today, with 18 Metroparks reservations, the Cleveland Metroparks Zoo, and more than 150 parks and playgrounds managed by the Cleveland Department of Parks, Recreation and Properties, it's no wonder so many locals have fond memories of the parks. Whether you refer to the facility as the Metroparks or the nearly 70-mile Emerald Necklace of paved trails, chances are you've got memories that took place somewhere in this vast green space. Add those memories to all the ones from suburban parks, and it's easy to see why summer is synonymous with outdoor activities.

BIG BIKE RIDE

The day before my first full-time job, my friends decided we should go for a bike ride along the Emerald Necklace. Little did I know that this was a 70-mile trek along the Metroparks Reservations (Chagrin to Rocky River)! —*Sally Slater Wilson*

NET RESULT: Summer fun in 1980 included playing volleyball in the Cleveland Metroparks.

WADING FOR A BIG WAVE:
The wading pool, Rocky River Reservation, 1951.

REFLECTING BY THE POOL:
The wading pool at Mastick Road picnic ground, Rocky River Reservation, 1950s.

THE VALLEY

We have memories of lots of activities in Cleveland Metroparks, *i.e.*, "the valley." We remember picnics, fishing, hiking, and exploring. We enjoyed the wading pool in the Mastick Picnic Area. —*Karl and Laura Riccardi*

RAINBOW IN ROCKY RIVER

Rocky River had nice parks for us kids to play in. We were allowed to walk to these parks at a very young age to play on the playgrounds without adult supervision. One fun game I remember was trying to knock each other off the teeter totter with "cherry bumps." We got hurt a lot, but that was part of the fun.

Elmwood Park was a great place to have a pick-up baseball game or toss around a Frisbee. When we were in high school, tons of us hung out in the woods there at a place we called Rainbow. Rainbow was in the woods at the back of Elmwood Park, by the ball fields. We would walk back along the railroad tracks and cut back in the woods to get to Rainbow. We would meet there for cookouts and bonfires. I think just about any kid from Rocky River in the '70s would know about Rainbow. —*Noreen Hone*

BIKING IN BRECKSVILLE

When we moved to Brecksville in 1958, we had access to the Metropark, which was literally down the road. Bike riding there was wonderful because you had the long hills, huge shaded tree areas, different pavilions, and there was a stream. Bike riding there was always an adventure, and quite a contrast from riding bicycles in a city atmosphere.
—*Dennis Gaughan*

LIFE LESSONS ON THE PLAYGROUND

There was nothing better than hanging out at the local city playground in the summer. These were staffed by college students. We called the guy "Coach" and the girl "Teach." It was a wonderful way for future teachers to get some training and to be paid for it at the same time. You could play softball for your playground against other city playground teams, train and complete in the Junior Olympics, or do crafts with "Teach" or hoops with "Coach."

My playground was at Memorial Elementary School on E. 149th St. I was there every weekday,

BRIDLE PARTY: Horseback riding in Big Creek Reservation, 1951.

TRAILBLAZERS: Hikers enjoy Chagrin Reservation, 1975.

and my younger brothers went there, too. A favorite memory was that each year at the end of the season, we always threw "Teach" in the pond—the Memorial pond, which honored those who died in the Collinwood School fire. We'd plan this event for weeks, trying to figure out a way to get her close to the pond so we could get her in. Too bad Cleveland no longer seems to have these playgrounds. We learned about sportsmanship, fair play and getting along with others—so much of which helped me throughout my life. And, yes, Grovewood was our biggest rival and the only place close where we could go to a public pool to swim. Talk about conflict! —*Toni Oliverio*

INSPIRED BY TARZAN

When I was a kid, my street dead-ended at the Metroparks' Big Creek Parkway. A gang of us kids played all summer in the creek, building dams and making cozy caves in the brush where we pretended we were "camping out." In one area there were ropy vines that hung from the trees, and we would climb up to a high branch, grab on and swing, yelling like Tarzan, trying to swing from tree to tree. I can still feel the blisters and splinters. If our mothers had known how dangerous a game it was, we would never have been allowed in the park again. —*Kathleen Cerveny*

RESERVATIONS ARE NECESSARY: We headed to parks like the North Chagrin Reservation for Memorial Day picnics, like this one in 1973.

"We would climb up to a high branch, grab on and swing, yelling like Tarzan."

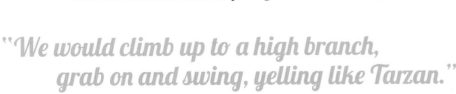

CLEVELAND CULTURAL GARDENS

I would often walk all the way to the lake, and then back up through Rockefeller Park. I was impressed by all of the nationality gardens. There were such wonderful sculptures in so many of them, really wonderful to see. I enjoyed the idea that people of different nationalities would come down there. Sometimes, in those days, they'd come down in costumes and put on little performances. So you'd see Polish dancers, for instance, in traditional Polish costumes on some particular weekend of the year. I loved seeing those nationality groups with their native costumes. I thought that was fascinating. —*Sam Bell*

SCARY SKATEBOARDING

In the early 1970s, the first bike path was paved in the valley (which is what we always called the Metroparks Rocky River Reservation). I rode my bike on it almost every day, a 10-mile round-trip before the length of the path was extended in later years. Skateboarding was very popular, and my brother and I decided to skateboard down the steepest hill on the path. The danger made the challenge more fun. We both made it to the bottom of the hill, knowing we would have been seriously hurt if we had fallen on the way down. I think the fear of death is what prevented us from ever trying that exhilarating escapade again. —*Laurie Ghetia-Orr*

CATCHING CRAYFISH

The gang and I loaded up our bikes early in the morning and we'd take the big ride to Euclid Creek. From our house in University Heights, we could go down to Green Road, all the way down to Anderson and then to the creek. There was a swimming hole there and we'd swim. We'd bring little plastic containers or jars and we would catch crayfish. They looked like lobsters, you know, about three inches long. That was a great swimming hole. —*Steve Presser*

KNOWING THE DRILL: Everybody gathered in the valley (aka Rocky River Reservation) for sports, recreation, picnics, and an all-around good time, circa 1970.

HOGSBACK HILL

The Riverside Drive entrance to the Metroparks' Rocky River Reservation was my gateway to a summer time-capsule of sorts. In my preschool years, my dad would drive us down into the park's cooler temperatures from the Detroit Avenue entrance and, if the gate was open, would cap off our ride with a left halfway up the hill at Riverside to visit the riding stables there. By the time I was counting down to summer breaks at McKinley Elementary School, a drive around the Stinchcomb-Groth Memorial built on the former site of the stables signaled our ride's end. During summers off from Horace Mann, my friends and I would ride our bikes there, then rocket down the hill everybody called "Stinchcomb" on the Hobie skateboards we'd brought with us. Summertime during my Lakewood High days included flying control-line model airplanes in the shadow of the memorial. I visited the hill often to fly kites during summers home from Ohio University. Around the time I-90 pushed through Lakewood, the northwestern slope of the hill was augmented with fill. (I know this because I threw a stick over the edge for my golden retriever to fetch and he brought back a red paving brick!) I learned years later that "Stinchcomb" was actually named Hogsback Hill and that it overlooks the first tract of land purchased by the guy on the monument for Cleveland's metropolitan parks system in 1919.
—George Ghetia

SLIDING INTO SUMMER: In the 1950s, children celebrated the arrival of summer at Cleveland Metroparks playgrounds.

AS POLLIWOGS GREW INTO FROGS IN SOUTH EUCLID

The southern part of Greenvale Road was lined with thick woods, ponds, and open fields. The city had yet to build duplexes and a public pool on what used to be an old bluestone quarry. One summer, one of the "bad boys" in the neighborhood stole a mixing tub from the South Euclid Cement Company on Green Road. He put it in the largest pond, discovered that it floated and took kids for rides, steering it with a long branch he would dip in the water. Sometimes, a kid could be alone for whole afternoons just looking at minute water life near the edge of one of the smaller ponds along that quiet road. As a six-year-old, I learned to love saying "polliwog", a word whose syllables ran to the beat of a horse gallop. I learned about how frogs grow just from watching, and learned just how long I could stand stagnant stink before I had to get up and wander back home. —Bunny Breslin

LOCATION, LOCATION, LOCATION: The Hotel Westlake was just one of the Rocky River attractions along the water.

Wild Things

Encounters with local wild-life left lasting impressions for city and suburban kids.

FROG FAN

I'm a big frog catcher. To this day, although I appreciate what John Carroll University has done with its expansion, where they built Don Shula Stadium was the last frog pond in the neighborhood. I have a photo of me holding two frogs in my neighbor's yard, probably in 1964. I loved catching frogs. I always had toads in my garage. I would create these boxes and things like that. But frogs were really, really cool. Sadly, in University Heights, back in the day, there weren't too many places to catch frogs.

—*Steve Presser*

THINGS THAT GO CRUNCH

One vividly icky memory was almost having a panic attack while tromping ankle-deep through the crispy exoskeletons of locusts in one particularly robust 17-year cycle.

—*Kathleen Cerveny*

OLD STATION ROAD

The year was 1977. I was 12. We lived a few hundred feet from Lake Erie in Lakewood in a house with no A.C. The August air was completely still and thick with humidity. Lake bugs swarmed and buzzed. Dad and I were sitting in the backyard, steaming in the heat as dusk fell.

"Come on," Dad said, "let's go for a drive."

Dad didn't tell me where we were going and I didn't ask. I just basked in the air turned magically cool by the car's motion, my hand sticking out of the passenger side window like a tiny bird swooping up and down in the draft.

The air along the Shoreway smelled of the lake and of Cleveland's acrid industry as we sped down I-77 past Republic Steel. We headed south and away and finally exited in Brecksville. Dad turned onto Old Station Road, which wound down the bank of the Cuyahoga River Valley. We parked.

"Listen," said Dad as we stepped out of the car.

The air was electric with the undulating chant of crickets. The tangled trees and vines were secrets against the indigo sky. Perspiration beaded on my lip. Dad drew disappearing red circles with the glowing tip of his Marlboro.

It took a few minutes for them to start, but start they did. The deepest loudest croaking I had ever heard.

"What is it?" I asked, my spine straightening.

"Bullfrogs."

"Jeez!"

We listened to the whole beautiful orchestra while Dad finished his beer. Then he took one long last drag of his cigarette and dropped the butt in the empty Stroh's can.

"Time to head on back," he said.

Old Station Road is cordoned off now. I've defied the NO TRESPASSING sign, but I've never found the bullfrogs again. Maybe they moved. Maybe they died.

Maybe it's time to look for them again.

—*Erin O'Brien,* Author of The Irish Hungarian Guide to the Domestic Arts

"The air was electric with the undulating chant of crickets."

Camp Experiences

The summer camp tradition—day camps as well as resident camps—brought with it a variety of outdoor experiences, to which campers had varying responses. Like it or loathe it, summer camp always made quite an impression. Looking back, lanyard-making and bug-juice drinking usually didn't rank as high as horseback riding, swimming or ghost stories around the campfire. There weren't too many food complaints, but then, food always seems to taste better when you're outdoors. Bring on the s'mores.

BUG JUICE, BASEBALL, AND MORE

Some of us were fortunate enough to go to day camp and overnight camp. I went to Belvoir School Camp. We would all drink Dean's Dirty Dishwater, as we used to call it. It was a half-pint of milk.

Then, I got lucky. In fourth, fifth, and sixth grades I went to Camp Roosevelt, which was an overnight camp in Perry, Ohio. It felt like I was going three states away. Perry was right on the lake and it was the greatest. We did everything there: sailing, waterskiing, wake boarding, archery, riflery. Then we did all the other normal camping things. You would have tennis, kickball, soccer, softball, capture the flag. It was a camp that had been around since the '20s, run by the Lorimer family of Shaker Heights. It closed down,

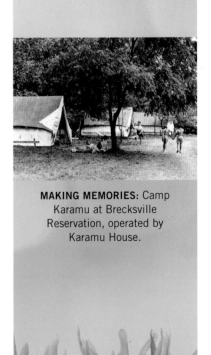

MAKING MEMORIES: Camp Karamu at Brecksville Reservation, operated by Karamu House.

Some Camp Snapshots

When speaking of their summer camp experiences, these were some of the camps Clevelanders mentioned.

CAMP ROOSEVELT FOR BOYS

1918–1987

Perry, Ohio

Camp Roosevelt, owned and operated by the Lorimer family, gave many Clevelanders lasting memories of horseback riding, swimming, and archery.

GREATER CLEVELAND COUNCIL OF THE BOY SCOUTS OF AMERICA

1919

Camp Wahema, Chagrin Reservation

This early Cleveland-area Boy Scout camp was acquired in 1919. The camp, along with other early Scout campsites, closed when the area became more populous. The Council now owns 1,200 acres at Camp Beaumont in Ashtabula County.

RED RAIDER CAMP

1933–1980

Russell Township

Red Raider was established by Ralston "Fox" Smith in the 1930s. By the 1970s, 600 campers from 30 area communities attended Red Raider during the summer months. The camp offered nature study, crafts, and horseback riding. It was sold to new owners in 1975, and in 1980 the property was sold to a developer.

and they donated the property to the National Parks. I went back for a reunion. It was honestly phenomenal.

At camp, you could go for two- or four-week sessions, or, if your parents really wanted to get rid of you, eight weeks. Four weeks was perfect. You slept in barracks, in bunks. I made great friends there. I was a pretty good athlete, so "Presser's Power House" was the name of our championship baseball team. You ate in the mess hall. You drank "bug juice," which is a great phrase. I think a lot of people call it bug juice. It really was just Kool-Aid-type juice. If you got it on your clothes, it stained. There was a camp uniform you had to wear. It was a white shirt with a blue emblem. My wife Debbie's father went there, and was also a camp counselor there.

We did mischievous things. It was heaven. Honestly, it was the greatest. A lot of my friends went there, and guys from other schools went there, and from the Temple. Mainly it was a Jewish camp, but there were a lot of non-Jewish people. Can you imagine being a kid and shooting a rifle and doing archery and waterskiing? It was fantastic, a great, great camp.

—*Steve Presser*

CAMPFIRES AND GHOST STORIES

I attended Red Raider overnight camp in the summers, and it was a great time—once I got used to being away from home. Of course, around the campfire I was terrified by the stories of the ghostly Red Raider who angrily wandered the woods with his lantern glowing blood red. —*Christine Howey*

MAKING ITS MARK: At Camp Roosevelt for Boys, activities included marksmanship instruction.

THE SWIM TO CANADA

Like most aging children of the Cleveland suburbs, I retain vivid memories of the yearly fortnights I spent, in company with my brothers, at summer camp. And, like many of our Catholic peers, our two-week sojourns were spent at Camp Isaac Jogues, a 33-acre plot of greenery perched on the Lake Erie shore in Madison.

Most of my camp memories are probably typical: inept craft sessions, interminable twilight softball games, campfire sing-alongs and all the kindred rituals ever invented to showcase our childish incapacities for virtually everything to an audience of our sneering peers and sniggering counselors. I particularly recall an attempt at making a leather wallet, which disintegrated at its first opening, and the assembly and decoration of a plastic goldfinch model, which, in my artistic hands, emerged looking like it had been hit by a large automobile. The nightly softball games were worse—the unathletic personal backgrounds of the Bellamy boys left us without the skills to perform adequately, much less excel, at any sport. So I spent a lot of time taking called third strikes and, in the unlikely chance I got on base, being thrown out in humiliating rundowns.

But there are good memories, too, and it would be unfair to suppress them. The food wasn't bad, except for the invariable tapioca dessert. Each day's activities climaxed with an awe-inspiring vespers service in the camp chapel, highlighted by the show-stopping Gregorian chanting of our counselors. Our male counselors, you see, were actually Catholic seminarians—Catholic priests in training—and the haunting beauty of their singing remains a beautiful memory even half a century later.

But I digress. Memory lane is often an ill-lit thoroughfare, but I believe it was during the summer of 1957 that those same Catholic seminarians gave me my first and most memorable tutorial in mob psychology. Our counselors, already practiced in the manipulation of malleable young minds, began with a fiendishly effective gambit designed to identify and target the most psychologically vulnerable among us. And so it was that what we came to call simply "The List" appeared on our cabin bulletin board the morning after we arrived at camp. It was short and to the point:

VOLUNTEERS WANTED! TO SWIM LAKE ERIE FROM CAMP ISAAC JOGUES TO CANADA! ONLY THE STRONG WILL SURVIVE! ARE YOU BRAVE ENOUGH? ARE YOU MAN ENOUGH? THIS ULTIMATE TEST OF MANLINESS AND COURAGE WILL TAKE PLACE ON SATURDAY MORNING AT 6 A.M. SIGN UP HERE!

Now, I only had to see "The List" but once to realize two things, both of them disquieting. The first was that I was neither brave nor man enough to swim to Canada, which I knew to be 60 miles distant, not to mention the fact that I didn't know how to swim. The second was that I would prefer

(continued)

CAMP HAPPINESS

Catholic Charities' Camp Happiness offers day camps at three locations—Parma, Lakewood, and Wickliffe—for the developmentally disabled.

CYO CAMP/CAMP ISAAC JOGUES

1945–1991

Madison

This CYO (Catholic Youth Organization) resident camp was established in 1945 and by the 1950s, more than 1,500 campers had attended the camp in Madison. In 1970, it was renamed Camp Isaac Jogues.

HIRAM HOUSE CAMP

1896-present

Ohio's oldest camp is also one of the 12 oldest camps in the United States, offering kids a chance to try their hand at boating, archery, crafts, and more.

IN THE SWIM: It was cool at Camp Roosevelt Pool.

BACK LAB: Skylab parties were all the rage in the summer of 1979, as we wondered where it would come back to Earth.

to die or be tortured like Isaac Jogues himself (who, as all good Catholics know, had so many of his fingers nibbled away by the Iroquois that he needed special Papal dispensation to handle the Host during Mass) than demonstrate to the counselors and my fellow campers that I was . . . afraid . . . to . . . swim . . . to Canada. I signed up immediately.

The four days until Saturday passed quickly. And what on Monday had seemed like some sort of harmless playground dare had metastasized by Thursday into a gnawing, shameful, and—it must be said—bowel-constricting terror. The final 36 hours were sheer torture, my intense fear of drowning being constantly trumped by my greater terror of being publicly exposed as the groveling coward I indubitably was. Friday night, the eve of this childhood Armageddon, was the worst. I lay sleepless and fidgeting until probably 4 a.m., quaking with panic as the H-Hour of my personal D-Day approached. Suffice it to say that if cowards, indeed, die a thousand deaths, I set new records in personal mortality that unforgettable night.

Came the dawn, and the swim volunteers—we brave, we unhappy few—stumbled outside in our bathing trunks to the lakeside assembly point . . . only to be informed that our swim had been cancelled, owing to some "technical" circumstances, which were appropriately couched and which I can no longer recall. But nothing mattered, anyway, because I knew, in that first instant after the announcement was made, that I had not only escaped being unmasked as the craven poltroon I was, but, even better, had inexplicably won public certification of my manliness. After all, if I was brave enough and tough enough to swim Lake Erie (and I was, wasn't I? Hadn't I signed up for it?), it was hard to say what I couldn't or wouldn't do or dare.

My bogus sense of elation did not last long, however. It would be nice to say that the ordeal had taught me a lesson in how to not let oneself get shamed into imprudent courses of action by fear of what others might think. But no, my evasion of the that first and most ridiculous test of manhood only set me up for an even worse ordeal the following week: my still-legendary debut in the camp prizefighting ring, an arena for achievement for which I was even less suited than the waters of Lake Erie. Youth, indeed, is wasted on the young. —*John Stark Bellamy II*

S'MORES OUTDOORS

I remember Brownie Day Camp in the valley (Rocky River Reservation of the Metroparks). My mom was one of the leaders and I went along, since my sister was a Brownie. We did crafts and ate s'mores. —*Laura Riccardi*

SCOUTS GET OUT

I was an Eagle Scout as a kid. I still am. Our troop met at 86th and Wade Park in the Methodist church. It took me all the years I was in the Scouts to become an Eagle Scout. You had to have 21 merit badges; some were required, and some you could choose. They covered a multitude of things. In high school I was already studying architecture, so I did the Architecture merit badge, and then went on to study architecture in college. Other boys did the same thing; they found something they liked and proceeded with it.

The scout camp for the local council was near Chagrin Falls, the South Chagrin Reservation, which was what we always called it, but its real name was Wahema, an Indian name. I learned that as an adult working at the Boy Scout museum here. Sixty years later, you learn something about your youth. The museum is the Nathan L. Dauby Boy Scout Museum, named for the general manager of The May Company department stores. The museum is in the lobby of the Greater Cleveland Council, Boy Scouts of America Service Center, at 22nd and Woodland Avenue. I'm an assistant curator. People bring in stuff they still have from when they were kids—patches, badges, neckerchiefs, old tents, uniforms, troop flags and anything else that had to do with the program.

One thing I remember is that my first train ride was with the Boy Scouts, from Cleveland to Wellington. We packed our things at the church, jumped on a bus to the Terminal Tower, got on a train to Wellington, and then from Wellington, we had to hike to our campsite. —Tony Macias

ONE TIME ONLY

When I was seven years old I had my first and last experience with summer camp. My parents managed to send all five of their children to Hiram House Camp for a session. I don't know whether it was one or two weeks, but it was an experience I never wanted to repeat. After the stomach-dropping ride south on S.O.M. Center Road, my parents dropped us off and quickly made their getaway, probably wondering how they had managed to pull off the feat of time away from all their kids, ages seven through 18. They pointed me toward the designated sign on a tree marked "girls, age 7" and peeled away. I was the first for my age to arrive at that spot and stood there alone and miserable until the counselor showed up. My brothers were off to their age-appropriate trees and my sister was a counselor that summer. I only saw them across the room at mealtime, or briefly during the walks from

CAMP FOLLOWERS: New arrivals at Hiram House Camp follow their counselor in 1959.

the cabins to the recreation periods. I had never slept away from my house before and my extreme shyness was a definite drawback.

My age group was assigned to a large dormitory cabin. In having to change clothes in front of others on your bunk, using toilet stalls that had hundreds of moths clinging to every surface (yes, the toilet seats, too!), using a flashlight to go to the bathroom at night and being feasted upon by mosquitos, my worst nightmare was realized. The swimming activities were fun, but the high diving board looked as tall as a building and scared the willies out of me. Casual, temporary friendships were created with girls whom I would never see again. The food was decent, but the experience certainly wasn't the fun adventure that other kids later recounted as the highlight of their summer vacation. The bonfire event inside the fort area on the last night was the most fun activity. The monstrous fire, the dramatic presentation, the singing, all the kids in one place at once . . . it helped wash away some of terror-filled nights with creepy crawlies in the inky-black cabin. —*Nicole Loughman*

FISH PHASE: Scenic Park in Rocky River Reservation drew a crowd of regulars who fished there, 1960.

DAY CAMP MEMORIES

One of the summer memories I have is going to day camp in the early '60s, at the Kiwanis cabin by Rockcliff Springs, in the valley (Rocky River Reservation). The cabin is long gone now. It was the Lakewood YMCA day camp when I was 9, 10, and 11 years old. The first year I went was in 1961; the last year was 1963.

It was just a cabin that we hung out at. We had BB guns and archery, played baseball across the street in the field, made birdhouses out of Popsicle sticks, and every week or two we'd go on a mystery trip. I remember three of them. We went to Malley's, seeing those big stainless steel vats filled with chocolate, and you just wanted to dive in. We also went to Coca-Cola on the East Side, and to Eveready, which was a battery factory, so they didn't have any pop or candy there.

At the end of every day we went swimming at the Lakewood Y. I think they wanted to send all of the kids home clean. Recently, I got a call from a guy I met at day camp 52 years ago. We're still friends. Six years after we stopped going to day camp, in the summer of 1969, we were both counselors at the same camp. It wasn't the same—there were no BB guns or archery. Every week on Thursday nights we had a camp-out, a Y event, at the cabin in the valley. We had big campfires. It seems like it never rained, for some reason.

In the valley, we watched people fish. Nobody ever caught anything. At day camp we fished off the river ford, and nobody every caught anything. We'd turn over rocks and find crayfish, though. We would go down to the river and that was where I learned to skip stones. Back then the Rocky River was really polluted. We never went in the river. —*Dave Davis*

HOT AND HUMID

In the summer between eighth and ninth grade, I volunteered at Camp Happiness, a camp for mentally challenged children. The days in Lakewood were hot, lazy, and long. No one had air conditioning in their cars or homes. We sometimes had a cool breeze from Lake Erie, but those were usually followed by a storm. I remember it being so humid that after showering and drying off, I would be soaked again before I finished dressing. —*Helen Wirt*

CAMPING IN KIRTLAND

Or should that be Kamping with a "k"? In 1955, *The Cleveland News* featured an article about a camping trip in which 15 kids took their fathers camping in Kirtland. *Cleveland News* editorial writer Paul Myhre aptly named the group "The News Benevolent Trenching, Tent-Toppling and Where's the Can-Opener Association." This adventurous group gathered their bamboo fishing poles and Davy Crockett Flashlights and headed for the Maynard Murch Farm in Kirtland for a well-documented camping experience.

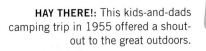

HAY THERE!: This kids-and-dads camping trip in 1955 offered a shout-out to the great outdoors.

HANGING AROUND: The Rotor at Euclid Beach Park, where the room spun and the floor dropped away, 1957.

WE WERE AMUSED

Tickets to Ride: Amusement Parks

EUCLID BEACH ATTRACTIONS: Eat, dance, laugh, and experience rides like the Rock-O-Plane.

While it is probably accurate to say that most people think the amusement park of their childhood was one of the best, there is also a good chance that Northeast Ohioans have valid reasons for thinking that. With so many amusement parks nearby, it is small wonder we grew up thinking the shores of Lake Erie were Roller Coaster Central. And you know what? We were right. For more than a century, Ohio has offered a wealth of amusement parks. Back in 1912, Ohio's 54 amusement parks were a number exceeded only by New York with 62 amusement parks and Pennsylvania with 61.

Luna Park (35 acres in the Woodland Avenue-Woodhill Road-East 110th Street-Mt. Carmel area) opened on Cleveland's East Side in 1905. In its day, it was a popular place offering rides, a roller rink, a dance hall and even a stadium. By 1929, however, the park was closed. In 1905, White City Amusement Park on East 140th St. featured the Shoot-the-Chutes boat ride, a fun house, the Scenic Railway roller coaster, a ballroom and more. After a fire in 1906, and storm damage the following year, the park closed in 1908. On the West Side was Puritas Springs Park, with its signature Cyclone Coaster. This park opened in 1898, and later, advertisements promoted the fact that it was close to the airport. It also has the dis-

NEW WAVE: It seems that each generation of Cleveland's children discovered the fun of Euclid Beach with boat rides, coasters, and carousels. The Mill Chute, opened in 1949, offered children a tame version of Over the Falls.

OPEN AIR GAMES AT EUCLID BEACH, 1960s: Group picnics at Euclid Beach often included games for the kids.

tinction of being the place where Jungle Larry made his amusement park debut with Jungle Larry's T.V. Circus. Puritas Springs Park closed in 1958. These days, though, the biggest memory-generators seem to be Euclid Beach Park, Geauga Lake Park and Chippewa Lake.

Are We There Yet?

In the summer, we headed for amusement parks on the bus, on trolleys, or in cars with kids in the back seat, filled with anticipation.

EUCLID BEACH PARK

Its policy of free admission, an assortment of activities, and the expansive picnic area drew crouds to Euclid Beach Park each year. The Humphrey family purchased Euclid Beach Park in 1901, and determined its no-alcohol policy and the system of using tickets rather than cash. With the credo of nothing to depress or demoralize, the park was ideal for family outings, reunions, company or association picnics and get-togethers with friends. Locals drove there, took public transportation, walked over from their Euclid Beach cottages, or found creative ways to get themselves to the park. No matter how you got to the park at East 156th and Lakeshore, for many, the anticipation-filled journey was part of the fun.

GETTING THERE WAS HALF THE FUN

My friend Dan and I had to have been 8 or 9 years old when we wanted to go to Euclid Beach. We rode our bikes there from Lakewood, on the shoulder of the Shoreway, because that was the only way I knew to get there. I knew the exit and everything. We went early in the morning, and never even told our parents. It was a big adventure. I didn't think we'd ever get there. It was a really windy day, and riding on the Shoreway shoulder I was thinking, "We're not supposed to be here." But there were no cops, and nobody stopped us. —*Steve Horniak*

TRY TO TOP THIS

Our family doctor, Dr. Wilcox, invited our family to an event at Euclid Beach Park in the late 1950s. My husband had to work and couldn't go, so the doctor drove the rest of us in his convertible. It's the only time I've ever ridden in a convertible, and I'm in my eighties. —*Joann Rae Macias*

"I look down and see we are flying over Lake Erie."

SWEET ANTICIPATION

Driving to Euclid Beach in the two-tone Olds '88 takes forever, my brother Jeff and I giggling in the back seat, reminding each other of the rides we'll tilt and twirl like the Bug and the Dippy Whip, what fun we'll have colliding with each other's Dodgem cars. We gaze up at the filigreed mazes of the Thriller and the Racing Coaster, listening to their clatter. Dad lugs a woven wooden picnic basket and a maroon battery radio. Mom carries a tablecloth and a Thermos of sugary iced tea, starred with quartered lemons and mint leaves from the garden. Dad stops at the ticket booth and buys a slew of curved paper tickets. He gives us yellow-wrapped candy kisses, sweet pink cotton candy fluff on paper cones, and sticky popcorn balls. We wait in line at Laff in the Dark, hearing shrieks and clamor. The lurching car we sit in bumps doors and monsters. Ticking up the tracks like a time bomb, the Aero Dips roller coaster with the electric smell pauses at the top before it plummets, whipping back my hair. We stop at the Penny Arcade to play skee ball. Jeff just misses treasures like golden rings as he directs the iron claw. He finally scoops up a marble and a stick of gum. At the Fun House, Laughing Sal keeps laughing, laughing, laughing, and mirrors ripple our bodies. Walking over a curved wooden floor I nearly lose my balance. The tinkle of the merry-go-round beckons and soon we are perched in the saddles of Great American Racing Derby horses. The silver rocket ship glides above the treetops, and we hear the echo of organ music from across the park. I look down and see we are flying over Lake Erie. At a picnic table near the water, we eat fried chicken. Then in the yellow-lit evening we wander over to the Pavilion Dance Hall, and inhale the sweaty smell of the open-air ballroom as we gape at men and women slow-dancing close to one another, holding on for their lives. —Linda Goodman Robiner

TOOK OFF LIKE A ROCKET: The bullet-shaped Rocket Ships had lasting appeal at Euclid Beach, as the ride evolved from The Circle Swing to The Airplanes to The Rocket Ships.

TAKING TURNS: Flying Turns at Euclid Beach, 1946, offered a taste of the bobsledding experience.

SUMMER JOB ON SHOOT THE RAPIDS AT CEDAR POINT

We lived in barracks called The Shingles. When you first started working at Cedar Point, they gave you these little training sessions, about three of them. The one that stands out the most in my mind is the one on courtesy. It was one of the old carousel slide shows with some sort of narration: "Treat the people nicely. Keep a smile on your face."

At one point, when I was loading people on the Shoot the Rapids boat, I handed my friend Patrick a camera. He was walking around the deck where I was loading people. I pulled a boat up and said, "Okay, when this boat goes I want you to get in the boat as quickly as you can, because I'm going to have to move you along." Meanwhile, on the other side of the deck, Patrick was very nonchalantly walking around with the camera. I made sure I had two boats ready, so I could shove the one out and get the next one ready. I got the next one up, and everyone cooperated. They jumped in, and the last guy was standing there: I just grabbed his shirt and bunched it up, and said, "Get in there." It happened much quicker than I can tell it: There's a perfect picture of me doing that. Then, I neatened up his shirt, and put him in. The reaction of the people in the boat was like, "What?" Two seconds later, everybody was laughing because they were in on the joke.

—Joe Gunderman

Has Anybody Seen My Gal?

She's about six feet tall, is missing a front tooth, and she's always laughing. Bigger-than-life Laughing Sal drew huge crowds of park-goers at Euclid Beach Park. She wasn't the only attraction, though. Everybody seemed to have a favorite ride.

LAUGHING SAL'S LASTING IMPRESSION

When I was three or four years old I thought children were children and grown-ups were grown-ups, and I was very happy to be a child because I got to play all the time instead of working like the grown-ups did.

I flash-forward to moving to the United States when I was seven or eight years old, with my first introduction to an amusement park. My first introduction to Euclid Beach Park was Laughing Sal. I was drawn to her because she never stopped laughing—she never had a frown. She just continually entertained. And I thought, "Wow! This is better that the clowns I used to see back in Austria at carnivals." They continually had to work, and this woman was just mechanical. You just pressed a button, and she went all day. —Leo Michitsch

EUCLID BEACH 1963

I am eight, my brother is six, and my cousins are all in between. The tradition was Nickel Day at Euclid Beach. Our Great Grandma Edna looked frail, barely five feet tall. But once a year, on Nickel Day, she seemed to come alive and would leave the house. Grandma Edna would sit under what seemed to me to be an enormous tree, near Laughing Sal. She would perch herself on a black wrought iron bench that encircled the tree, with her black purse on her lap. The magic purse, as we called it, spewed tickets non-stop all day long. We would run back and forth, saying, "More tickets, Grandma." Her tiny hands, wearing black lace gloves to protect her from any sun, gleefully handed us those tickets. The highlight for us was when she would ride on the carousel with us. She did not ride on a horse. She rode on one of the ornate bench seats. We kept looking back at her the entire time: "Look at me, look at me." The drums of the carousel boomed in our ears and the music was unforgettable. I look back now and think that maybe I was in heaven during those three or four minutes . . . The smells, the sounds, cousins, brother, and me, all tanned, happy and sticky from custard cones and candy kisses. —Renee Hanna Irvin

ROTOR RECOLLECTION

My brother Steve and his friend Butchie took me to Euclid Beach, and I was so thrilled. They were 16 or 17 and I was 11, about the time I had a small crush on Butchie. They were going and offered to take me. I couldn't believe how generous that was—especially because we didn't get along that famously after I had taken my brother's piggy bank years earlier.

I was so touched by their including me. They paid for my tickets, and I had a fabulous time. They took me to a place I'd been to dozens of times before, but it never had quite the feeling it did on that very special day. It was probably the last time I had any interaction with my brother's friend, who died shortly thereafter.

I remember the Rotor. I was always afraid that, because I was so light, it would grab my clothes and I'd slip out of them, and I would be embarrassed because I was a budding teenager. And I remember Laughing Sal's laugh. I always wished I could be that uninhibited with those giant belly laughs.

— *Nicole Loughman*

FREQUENT RIDER

One of the things we used to do every weekend was go to Euclid Beach. We lived in East Cleveland at the time, on Elderwood, and my Dad would walk to work at General Electric. We went to Euclid Beach almost every weekend, my dad, my mom, and my grandparents. I have a lot of fun memories there. Laughing Sal was my favorite—I was fascinated by her. I would stand and look at her, and laugh and laugh and laugh. I also loved riding the roller coasters and Flying Turns. My favorite ride was probably the Flying Turns. I loved the old Euclid Beach Carousel, too. —*Larry Fox*

**MIDWAY FOOD:
SOME FAVORITE TREATS**

- Euclid Beach: Cotton candy, popcorn balls, candy kisses, hot dogs, frozen whip

- Geauga Lake: Elephant ears, popcorn, caramel apples and peanuts

- Chippewa Lake: French fries with lots of salt and vinegar, cotton candy

(left)

HOW ABOUT A HAND FOR EUCLID BEACH? Standing in line for your favorite rides was sweet anticipation.

(right)

REACHING NEW HEIGHTS: Coasters at Euclid Beach were the ultimate.

THERE FOR FORTUNE:
Arcade machines at Euclid Beach in 1969 included the Fortune Teller.

RAVES FOR OUR FAVES: Their names changed, but the Chute/Over the Falls ride and the Derby Racer/Racing Coaster had staying power at Euclid Beach.

"The Chute" Over the Falls. Euclid Beach Park.

Cleveland, Ohio.

DERBY RACER, EUCLID BEACH.

HUNDREDS OF MEMORIES

I must have gone to the park at least 300 to 400 times from 1953 to 1969. What I remember was the Flying Scooters, nicknamed The Butterflies, The Bug, and the Rocket Ships. I saw the rocket ship riding around in the Tremont area in 2011. I also remember Over the Falls—you'd ride through a dark tunnel—and the Derby Racing Coaster. The first time I was on that was in 1953. They had a bargain day, when all the rides were 5 cents. There were the Thriller and the Flying Turns, too, but my favorite was the Dodgem. I also remember Grandmother Fortune and the laughing lady, Laughing Sal, outside the Fun House. They had popcorn, hot dogs and frozen custard, but my favorite was the candy kisses. They also sold a lot of hot dogs at Euclid Beach. —*George Popovich*

FAMOUS LINES

I went to Euclid Beach with the Lakewood Y—they had trips there. I remember the park being really old, but The Thriller and the Racing Coaster were excellent. I still see this vehicle that looks like an old Euclid Beach ride. It's a rocket car now. I've seen it twice in the last two weeks. Euclid Beach also had the Flying Turns ride that was like a bobsled. The Racing Coaster and the Thriller had the longest lines, though. —*Dave Davis*

ROCK-AND-RIDES

My summers growing up in Cleveland were spent visiting my grandfather's mother, who may have been "old," but held a magical key to "wonderland." You see, every summer, my snow-bird great-grandmother, Katherine Carter, rented a cottage at the most fun-filled place on earth—Euclid Beach Park. How lucky my brother Dennis and I were to have an "in" at the most popular amusement park in Northeast Ohio! It was our own version of Coney Island, perhaps more beautiful with its forest of Sycamore trees, whose leafy limbs hung over the jade-green park benches like protective canopies.

And against the backdrop of mobile homes and sturdy summer cottages, there was a sense of home. Particularly if you were one of the lucky ones, like us.

"Kiddie Land"—inside a large concrete building called The Colonnade—was a world made for children with its miniature versions of many of the bigger, more adult rides. But if I thought that was paradise as a child, I was in for far more thrills as a teenager . . .

In the 1960s, Euclid Beach hosted shows by popular acts of the day. And thanks to Grandma Carter, Dennis and I had a backstage pass. Sort of. The Lovin' Spoonful was performing there in the summer of 1967 on the heels of their big hit, "Summer in the City," and this thirteen-year-old had a huge crush on the band's drummer, Joe Butler.

And my really, really great-Grandma had connections. She not only got us tickets, we got to meet them because they were using the cottage next to hers for a dressing room. Imagine my glee as I stood outside waiting for them to emerge. Then the screen door opened and there he was! My Joe, looking right at me and actually talking to me! He was cute, charming, and oh so nice.

After getting his autograph, I mumbled a nervous thank-you before they were all whisked away in a limo toward the concert hall.

My teenage crush may have disappeared all too soon, but that summer memory has lasted forever. —*Deanna R. Adams, author of* Rock 'n' Roll and the Cleveland Connection

ROCK AND ROLL AND THE JUNGLE BEAT
"Jungle Larry" Tetzlaff wasn't everywhere, but there was a time when amusement park aficionados might have thought so. Clevelanders watched him every week on the *Captain Penny Show* on Channel 5. He milked rattlesnakes and introduced us to animals such as monkeys, alligators, tigers, and his two pythons, Rock and Roll.

In 1957 and 1958 Jungle Larry's Jungle Circus was also an attraction at Puritas Springs Park. In 1959, he relocated to Chippewa Lake Park and remained there until 1964 when Jungle Larry's Safari Island opened at Cedar Point. Jungle Larry and his wife Nancy spent 30 years at the Cedar Point location, completing their run there in 1994.

PRE DRIVER ED: The junior version of the Dodgem cars was an attraction at Geauga Lake, 1983.

Geauga Lake

As a summer resort (complete with amenities such as roller skating, a dance pavilion, a baseball diamond and a carousel), Geauga Lake opened in 1887. In 1925 it became the Geauga Lake Park we all remember today, with midway games and rides like Dodgem and The Whip. In later years, favorite rides included the Wild Mouse, the Flying Coaster, the Rockets, and The Clipper. In 1975, Geauga Dog became the park's mascot. Geauga Lake's name changed to Six Flags Ohio in 2000, and when SeaWorld of Ohio was purchased the following year, the result was Six Flags World of Adventure. In 2004, Cedar Fair (the parent company of Cedar Point) bought it, and restored its original name of Geauga Lake Park but it closed after the 2007 season.

The sensory bombardment of area amusement parks sticks in our minds as much as the rides, and Geauga Lake Park is no exception. Its sights, sounds, scents, and flavors have created colorful memories.

MAKING TRACKS FOR THE TILT-A-WHIRL: Park-goers at Geauga Lake headed for signature rides such as the Big Dipper, The Flying Coaster and the Tilt-A-Whirl.

HANGING OUT: Geauga Lake offered the exhilarating Paratrooper ride.

FLOATING ALONG AT SEAWORLD: Boat rides appealed to kids who visited there in 1988.

SCENTS, SOUNDS, AND GOING AROUND

Some of my fondest childhood memories are of summer days spent at Geauga Lake in the '80s and early '90s. I remember not being able to sleep because I was so excited. As a child, the anticipation was as intense as what I felt Christmas Eve waiting for Santa. My first ride of the day was always the same—the Big Dipper. From there, I would laugh hysterically with my mom on Tilt-A-Whirl, rock out on Musik Express, and make myself dizzy on the Rotor. I can vividly remember walking along the boardwalk area and smelling popcorn, elephant ears, and sunscreen. The soundtrack was always a Beach Boys song along with the distant screams and rumbles from "The Wave." The rest of the day was usually spent on roller coasters. I remember one visit on a particularly slow day for the park. There was no line for the Corkscrew and we must have ridden it a dozen times in a row without ever getting off of it. On the way out, I always got a caramel apple with peanuts for the ride home. —*Emily Hitchcox*

GEAUGA LAKE ANTICIPATION

Sitting in school near the end of the school year, I was always waiting to go to Geauga Lake. I always felt privileged, knowing I could spend the summer not only in a wooded area with bikes, but having a train and an amusement park nearby. —*Dennis Gaughan*

"My first ride of the day was always the same–the Big Dipper."

COTTAGE INDUSTRY: Family members work on a Geauga Lake cottage in the 1950s.

OF COTTAGES AND COASTERS

We had a cottage at Geauga Lake in the early 1950s. The park was very old and had been there a long time. My husband was studying architecture, and he wanted to build a cottage from the ground up, so we bought a lot there. We lived in the cottage one year, year-round. We put in a cistern—the pipes froze, and we had no plumbing.

We loved the roller coasters at Geauga Lake. We called them "rollie coasters." It's so sad the park is gone. —*Joann Rae Macias*

COMPANY PICNIC

My father worked at TRW and in the 1950s, they had a picnic at Geauga Lake. The rides were free, and it was a lot of fun. —*George Popovich*

SEAWORLD SEAL OF APPROVAL

One year, my birthday present was to swim with the seals at SeaWorld. Most kids wanted to swim with the dolphins, but I thought they were kind of scary. I preferred swimming with seals, so I got all suited up in a wet suit and swam with the seals. I remember debating with my mother about whether seals had fur. I said they did, and I was right. They were very friendly, and brushed up against me in the water when I was swimming. When you swam with them, it was just you and the seals, a private swim. It was definitely worth it as a birthday gift. —*Molly Orr*

SEA THE WORLD: SeaWorld in Aurora gave us an up-close look at seals, Shamu the killer whale and other marine life.

How Moms Managed

Many families devised methods for keeping track of their kids in the vastness of Cedar Point. Here are two examples.

THE FABRIC OF SUMMER

I remember that my mom and some of the other neighborhood mothers in Berea got together and made all of the neighborhood children matching outfits to go to Cedar Point—so they could find us easily. The girls wore jumpers made out of red bandana material, and the boys wore red bandana shirts.

—*Lynette Macias*

TAKING A BREAK AT THE BREAKERS

When I was older, starting around age 10, I remember our annual trips to Cedar Point. My parents always got a room at the Breakers Hotel and would send us off to the park. There were anywhere from eight to 10 of us, and we used what my father called the buddy system. We were assigned a sibling and had to stay with that person all day. My dad would come out and ride a few rides and then go back to the hotel. My mom never came into the park. She would bring a good book and spend the day at the hotel. I thought she was crazy for missing all the fun. Now as an adult I understand this was a great day of relaxation for a mother of 11 children.

—*Peggy King-Neumann*

Ride 'Em!

Whether you sought the sense of anticipation as the roller coaster car ratcheted up on its ascent, or the sudden drop and the wind in your hair on the way down the hill, Clevelanders' lists of favorite rides at area amusement parks often include the following:

EUCLID BEACH FAVES

The Great American Racing Derby

The Flying Scooters (aka The Butterflies)

The Rocket Ships (bullet-shaped cars suspended from cables)

The Bug (that tossed you together with everybody else in your car)

Over the Falls (through a tunnel and up a hill before the boat splashed down into the water)

The Carousel

Racing Coaster (which of the two coasters would come in first?)

The Thriller (wooden roller coaster)

Flying Turns (a bobsled-like ride)

Laff in the Dark (lots of surprises as you headed into the dark in your car)

Dodgem (a smashing good time in this bumper car experience)

The Rotor (centrifugal force at work, when the floor of this barrel-like room drops down and you stuck to the sides of the walls)

The Turnpike (a driving ride)

Antique Cars (a driving ride)

Chippewa Lake Park

Located in Medina County, Chippewa Lake Park offered rides like the Big Dipper, the Little Dipper, the Wild Mouse, Bumper Cars, Flying Cages, and a Ferris wheel. In 1959, after Puritas Springs Park closed, Jungle Larry relocated to Chippewa Lake Park, where he acquainted park-goers with some of the animals they'd seen him with on the *Captain Penny* television show. He remained at Chippewa Lake until Jungle Larry's Safari Island opened at Cedar Point in 1964. Chippewa Lake Park also featured popular music. On Memorial Day weekend in 1966, for example, the park was the site of the first WIXY Appreciation Day (WIXY 1260-AM Radio), with bands such as The Beau Brummels on hand.

WHAT TO WATCH FOR

My grandfather worked for Dill Manufacturing, and they had their annual summer picnics at Chippewa Lake Park. We would spend the whole day just riding the rides. Their rickety old roller coaster there was my favorite. Everybody would put out all this food and take over the whole park. Everything was free. I was eight or nine years old, and had a stack of vouchers. Every half-hour, they would call numbers, and I won a Helbros men's wristwatch. At the time, it was probably worth about $100. It was too big for me, but I kept it. —*Larry Fox*

MORE CHIPPEWA LAKE MEMORIES

Although Chippewa Lake was a smaller park, they had one great feature that Geauga Lake didn't have—two great speedboats. For a dollar you could get a speedboat ride around Chippewa Lake at what seemed like very high speed. One of the speedboats was called "Firecracker." So you would bring your picnic baskets and lunch and dine inside this pavilion and then, of course, enjoy the rides in addition to the speedboats. I was always going on the train ride because that was so much fun. There was another called the Cover Up which was a Caterpillar ride that would start up, and then the tent would cover up everybody, and that was a lot of fun too. The roller coaster there was very small but exciting because it wound through a wooded area. And of course there was the ever-present cotton candy, and french fries with lots of salt and lots of vinegar. —*Dennis Gaughan*

CHIPPEWA LAKE COTTAGES

When you talk about Chippewa Lake, most people are nostalgic about the cottages. Families went to Euclid Beach or Puritas Springs for a day. When they went to Chippewa, you could go for day or an evening, but most people went there to rent cottages. That's what my family did. It's where I learned to swim. They also had games of chance, like the kewpie doll game, where you had to hit it with three baseballs in a row. My dad said Bob Lemon couldn't have done better. It was 1954, a rainy night, and the carny guy couldn't believe it. I hit the first one and he didn't pay any attention. I hit the second one, and then the third one. I picked the biggest prize I could. They also had a Caterpillar ride, and when you were riding, a cover came over it and you wondered what was going on. The other thing nice thing at Chippewa Lake was that you could have small boats there. —*William Kless*

Memphis Kiddie Park

Memphis Kiddie Park opened in 1952, and while it is still in operation today, it really left its mark on kids who frequented the park in the '50 and '60s.

THE OPENING

When Memphis Kiddie Park opened in 1952, my Uncle Al took me there. I was nine years old. —*George Popovich*

KIDDIE BOAT MISHAP

Growing up near Biddulph Plaza on the West Side, one of our family's favorite places for summer fun was the Kiddie Park on Memphis Avenue. It was a great place (and still is) for little ones to enjoy a variety of mini rides—all totally safe. That is, unless you happen to lean too far forward and bump your head on a steering wheel while on the boat ride, as I did. The experience left me with a souvenir—a small chip in my front tooth. —*Debbie Jancsurak*

(continued)

GEAUGA LAKE FAVES

Fun House	Tilt-A-Whirl (a spinning ride)
Dodgem	
Rocket Ships	The Rotor
The Clipper (later known as The Big Dipper)	Trabant (tilting, spinning circular ride)
Wild Mouse (small car roller coaster)	Spider (spinning spider-shaped ride)
Flying Coaster	Himalaya (circular ride)

CHIPPEWA LAKE PARK FAVES

The Big Dipper (wooden roller coaster)	Flying Cages (moved by shifting your weight)
The Little Dipper (junior version of the Big Dipper)	Ferris Wheel
The Wild Mouse	The Caterpillar (circular ride with a track and a canopy)

RIDES FOR POSTERITY: (From the top) The Mile High Cyclone at Puritas Springs Park, the Himalayan at Geauga Lake and the Flying Scooters at Euclid Beach.

MEMPHIS BLUE: Opened in 1952, Memphis Kiddie Park is now a local summertime institution.

KIDDIE PARKS

• Cleveland Zoo Kiddie Park, known for rides such as its railroad train, operated from the 1950s to the 1970s

• Kiddie Playland on Northfield Road in the vicinity of Randall Park Mall's later location, 1950s

• Memphis Kiddie Park opened in 1952

PLEASE REMAIN SEATED UNTIL THE RIDE COMES TO A COMPLETE STOP: PARK CLOSING DATES

• Luna Park 1929

• Puritas Springs Park 1958

• Euclid Beach Park 1969

• Chippewa Lake 1978

• Geauga Lake Park 2007

MEMPHIS KIDDIE PARK IN THE '60S

What a great place in the 1960s for kids and parents. We would head straight to the ticket booth and begin the adventure. My brother and sister are four years and six years older than I am, and were too big for the rides, so they would play in the game room and play miniature golf. They grudgingly rode the train as a family. It circled the park and had theme areas set up, like Snow White and the Seven Dwarves. The ticket booth was in a white building with red trim on the windows, with a live white poodle in the window. I always found a reason to get another ticket so I could see the poodle again, or eat my snow cone while staring at the poodle the whole time. I also loved the track with the small cars that you powered by pumping the bar back and forth. They later converted the pump handle to a round crank with handles. When I took my own kids to Memphis Kiddie Park 30 years later, I found it interesting that they, too, were afraid to ride the mini Ferris wheel and roller coaster at first. Later, these became their favorite rides.

—*Laurie Ghetia-Orr*

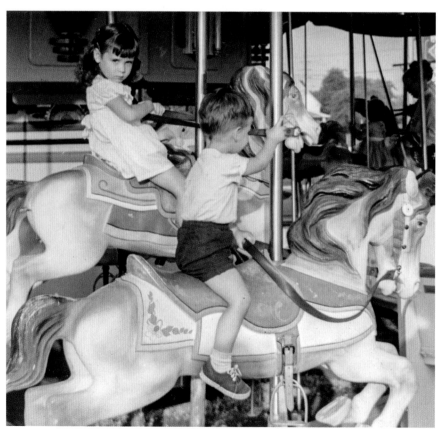

A HORSE APIECE: Memphis Kiddie Park merry-go-round, circa 1955. The park opened in 1952.

Summer Speeds By

The car culture left its mark on us, with drive-in restaurants and theaters, go-karts and auto races. We also had a fondness for railroad cars. Trains held a fascination for children, and because those trains were accessible, many kids of Cleveland have memories of riding on trains in the summertime.

The Disappearing Railroad Blues

For some kids, summer and trains just naturally seemed to go together, whether you paid for your ticket or found another way to ride. While we don't talk too much about trains these days, the experience certainly left its mark.

THE TRAIN YARD IN PAINESVILLE

My parents first met when they worked for the railroad in the 1940s. They both were ticket takers, selling tickets for the passenger trains at the Terminal Tower. Eventually they got married, and my mom, Rosemary Flynn, continued to work for the railroad as a train dispatcher until the 1970s. The people who worked for the railroad all ate lunch together at Harvey's; they called the waitresses Harvey Girls. The most famous person my mom ever sold a ticket to in the 1940s was W.C. Handy. He autographed the sheet music to "The Saint Louis Blues" for her. She was really happy to have his autograph on that because she was born in St. Louis.

I lived in Rocky River, and during the summers in the 1960s my mom would drop me off for the day at the train yard in Painesville where my father's cousin worked. He was the railroad engineer for the B&O Railroad (Baltimore & Ohio). I would spend the whole day there while he switched trains to different tracks and hooked the train cars up in the order they needed to be in to ship freight. I actually got to drive a locomotive with him when I was a kid. The fireman assigned to the train yard, along with my cousin and I, would make a day of riding in a railroad car. The fireman played harmonica, I played miniature banjo and we all sang songs together.

—*Patrick Flynn*

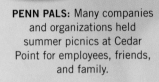

PENN PALS: Many companies and organizations held summer picnics at Cedar Point for employees, friends, and family.

"I actually got to drive a locomotive with him when I was a kid."

LOCOMOTIVE IN LORAIN

There was a park in Lorain that was home to a locomotive that I thought was really cool, out on Route 58 near the Southview area. —*Paul Negulescu*

A REAL TRAIN RIDE

Our family took a train ride from Rocky River to the Terminal Tower. Mom and Dad wanted my sister Sue and me to experience a real train ride. My brother wasn't born yet, so Sue and I were probably eight and six.
—*Laura Riccardi*

THE TRAIN TO CHIPPEWA LAKE

My Grandfather worked for Dill Manufacturing precision machinery company here in Cleveland. They always had their annual picnic at Chippewa Lake, and it was another day of adventure. The best part was that we got to take the train from Cleveland down to Chippewa Lake. That was another thrill, being able to ride the train—it was about an hour's train ride. These special picnic trains would let us off right near the train that Chippewa Lake ran. So you got off the real train and got on the park's train to ride into the park itself. —*Dennis Gaughan*

STEAM TRAIN ADVENTURE

In 1958, my brothers and I were members of a Cleveland Heights Cub Scout pack, and my mother was pressed into service as our pack leader. Channel 5 news analyst Dorothy Fuldheim and her husband, William ("Call me Uncle Bill") Ulmer were our next-door neighbors. Uncle Bill and my mother devised a wonderful summer field trip idea. He arranged a tour of one of the steam locomotives parked at the East 75th Street Small Engine Terminal of the Nickel Plate Railroad. The parked locomotives could be spotted by passengers riding the CTS rapid transit downtown from University Circle.

Many times I had seen the good guys battling the bad guys on the swaying roof of a steam train in westerns shown at the Fairmount Theater. At the train terminal, we gawked at the water tank, coal storage and large fuel tank for diesel locomotives. One by one, we climbed up into the steam locomotive and I ended up last aboard.

Flinching as a wave of heat blew out through the open doors of the firebox, I stared as the fireman shoveled coal into the inferno.

The train engineer turned to me and asked me if I wanted to start the train. I was stunned. The train was going to actually move and I was going to start it! "Kid, turn that valve." I looked where he was pointing, at a filthy-

RIDING THE RAILS

1920: The Shaker Heights Rapid Transit (Cleveland Interurban Railroad) begins service between Shaker Square and Public Square.

1930: Regular passenger train service opens at Cleveland Union Terminal and continues until 1977. Railroads included the Baltimore & Ohio, Big 4, Erie, New York Central and Nickel Plate.

1941: CTS (Cleveland Transit System) is established.

1954: Trackless trolleys and buses replace streetcars on Cleveland streets.

1955: The crosstown rapid transit line begins service between Cleveland Union Terminal and Windermere, and between the terminal and West 117th Street.

1968: Cleveland has the first rapid transit system in the U.S. connecting a major airport with a downtown business district.

1974: The Greater Cleveland RTA is established.

looking round handle. I turned the handle and the train started moving. I kept my hand glued to the valve in case I had to spin it quickly closed to stop the train and avert a tragic railroad accident. Little did I know that the engineer was actually controlling the train. At the time I was the happiest, most nervous kid in the world. Then the engineer blew the whistle and blew my mind. Casey Jones, look out! Years later my best friend Butchie Green and I would jump freight trains and ride Conrail Bridge #1 on summer evenings.

—Stephen Bellamy

LIFE ALONG THE TRACKS

Having grown up on the west side next to a patch of open woods flanked by the New York Central line, it's hard to think of summer as a kid without the smell of molten creosote oozing from the sun-burnt ties and the milkweed pods that lined the right of way. In short, my brother and I hung around the tracks—a lot.

We'd often lie in wait for a passing caboose (there were many then, often occupied) on the slow freights when we'd leap out, pleading "chalk . . . chalk . . . chalk" in screechy kid voices. Occasionally, the running crew rewarded our hectoring by tossing stubs of the jumbo sticks they used to mark freight cars, and those triumphant moments inevitably led to neighborhood graffiti jags.

And much to the eternal horror of parents everywhere, yes . . . we used to jump trains, often riding them down a half-mile or so to Sunrise Pool. Climbing signal towers and hiking up and sneaking into the abandoned Linndale passenger station were also good for some thrills.

But life on the rails had its risks. On at least one occasion, we got brought home by the railroad police, who lectured us in front of our parents about dismemberment (with suitably grisly photos) and life in "Juvie."

Grounded, we stuck to the yard for a few days. But the rails were magnetic, and we were fortunate enough to survive our future, sometimes darker, adventures along the tracks. —Mark Krieger

TRAIN GANG: A 1958 Cub Scout troop visit to a Nickel Plate Railroad steam locomotive.

FLICK PICKS: In June 1968, drive-in theaters were going strong in Northeast Ohio.

Car Culture

Summer sped by, especially if you were into car races, ranging from to stock cars to the Budweiser Cleveland 500 that first took place at Burke Lakefront Airport on July 4, 1982. The event that year offered $200,000 in prize money. Drag strips, go-kart tracks and speedways figured into our speedy summers, too. Another summer favorite car activity was going to drive-in movie theaters. Usually, there was just one movie choice at the drive-in, but in 1972 the Aut-O-Rama Drive-In in North Ridgeville became the Aut-O-Rama Twin Drive-In, offering customers a selection of movies.

DRIVE-IN MOVIES

The family-owned Aut-O-Rama Twin Drive-In on Lorain Road in North Ridgeville was opened by the Sherman family in 1965. Deb Sherman started working there in 1969, and later was president of the Aut-O-Rama Twin Drive-In for more than 19 years. Now her son Jim Sherman is president, and her son Del is vice president.

DRIVE-IN GENERATIONS

I started working at the Aut-O-Rama in 1969 as my first job, at the concession stand. I've done most of the jobs there, except anything mechanical. The beginning of the '70s was probably when you saw the maximum number of drive-in theaters in the Cleveland area. There were about 20 drive-ins back in the day.

I don't know that the experience itself has changed since the 1970s. It is an activity that people of all ages enjoy—kids, teenagers, adults, senior citizens. The biggest change has been in going digital. Before, the drive-in projectors were the original ones that theaters had when they opened. Pretty much, you changed the parts and nothing else really changed. Since we've gone digital, people come in and say it's like sitting in their living room watching a gigantic HD TV. It's a huge difference; people notice it because it's so much better. —*Deb Sherman*

Drag strips, go-kart tracks and speedways figured into our speedy summers.

TRUNK SHOW AT THE DRIVE-IN MOVIES

I remember going to the Memphis Road drive-in with my friends. To save money on the admission, two people would sit in front and the rest of us got in the trunk of the car. We then parked in the last row and three or four of us would exit the trunk and we would all watch the movie. Thank God cars were big back then. —*Peggy King-Neumann*

ENJOYING FAMILY NIGHT AT THE DRIVE-IN MOVIES

Drive-in movies were always my parents' way of entertaining us throughout the summer. We'd go early to play on the swings and other playground equipment in the front of the Euclid or Eastlake drive-ins. Mom would always make a big jug of Wyler's lemonade and it was a big treat to get the special popcorn from the concession stand. You always had to keep the window rolled halfway up to hold the speaker so you could hear the sound for the movie. Dad always remembered to put the speaker back in its cradle after the shows were over, but not everyone did. —*Donna "Dahmia" Komidar*

CUSTOMIZING THE BUICK

I remember the summer I painted my grandfather's brand-new car, a green late model Buick. They were painting his house, and I liked the paint color—kind of a cream coffee color. I had a huge stick, and I used it to drizzle paint all over his new car. When he saw it, I remember my grandfather used a lot of Hungarian swear words that I didn't understand. —*Howard Schwartz*

SHOPPING FOR A NEW PONTIAC

I have a photo of myself, taken at Arthur Pontiac. Every summer, my grandfather used to start thinking about a new car, and religiously, every two or three years, he had to have a new Bonneville. My favorite was a white one that had wood-grain paneling and a burgundy velour interior, with power buttons for everything. My grandfather would always start talking to Mr. Arthur late in the summer, and we'd go there for a big open house in the early fall, catered by Hough Bakeries. Arthur Pontiac was on the corner of Monticello and Mayfield roads in Cleveland Heights. —*Larry Fox*

ZOOM WITH A VIEW: Convertible season in Cleveland was also the time for car dealer promotional events.

THE CAR TO DRIVE in '65 IS AN ARTHUR PONTIAC

DRIVING FORCE: Jeff Iula, who later became general manager of the All-American Soap Box Derby, races in the 1966 All-American.

LIFE IN THE FAST LANE: *(below, left)* 1952 World Champion Joe Lunn was surrounded by celebrities (from left) Jimmy Stewart, Edgar Bergen and Joe E. Brown at the All-American Soap Box Derby in Akron.

1957 BIG WHEELS: *(below, right)* Celebrities Roy Rogers, Jimmy Stewart and George Montgomery competed in the '57 Oil Can Trophy Race during the All-American Soap Box Derby.

The All-American Soap Box Derby

Billed as the Greatest Amateur Racing Event in World, the All-American Soap Box Derby is held in Akron at Derby Downs each July. The first race was held in Dayton in 1934, but the event moved to Akron the following year. Each year, children from across the United States and beyond come to Northeast Ohio to race the cars they have built. Jeff Iula, former general manager of the All-American Soap Box Derby and co-author of the book *How I Saw It: My Photographic Memory of the Soap Box Derby*, shares his ideas about why the event has such staying power.

"There are several reasons the All-American Soap Box Derby is so special," he says. One of them is its host city, Akron. "It's been an Akron event since 1935. It promotes the city, plus brings in over $1.5 million every year to Akron. It's really 'Akron's All-American Soap Box Derby.' Akron gives a lot to the Derby, and the Derby gives to Akron. They don't run the Indy 500 in Chicago or the Kentucky Derby in West Virginia. The Derby is what Akron is known for," he says.

Iula also points to the fact that the Soap Box Derby is a tradition. "The Derby has had a long tradition of people building their cars, testing, running in rallies, winning their local races, coming to Akron, being welcomed, trial runs, meeting the other champs, the Topside Show, the parade, the race, the winners' circle, the awards show and going for the 'Gold Jacket.'"

Finally, he says, there's the family factor. "The Derby has been a family sport since the first year in 1934, when Bob Turner won the first race and his brother, Leo, helped him build the car. His mom and dad drove him to Dayton to win that first race. The Derby is now in its fourth generation of families. My dad ran

the Akron race for 20 years. I worked at the All-American as general manager for 35 years, my wife has volunteered for 21 years, my two kids and two nephews raced in the 1990s, and now my two grandkids are racing and won last year. The Derby is the third-longest-running car race in the United States, after the Indy 500 (1911) and Pikes Peak (1925)."

A FAMILY TRADITION, AND MORE

I couldn't come up with just one memory after 55 straight years of All-American Soap Box Derbies, starting in 1959. I have a lot of good memories. Some of my favorite Soap Box Derby memories are racing in the All-American as a sub in 1966, and my best friend and next-door neighbor, Billy Ford, winning the Akron local in 1970. My nephew Chris Roberts won the Indy local in 1988, the first time our family ever won. I got engaged to my wife, Nancy, at the Derby Awards Show in 1989; we've now been married 23 years. In 1992, my second nephew, Matt Roberts, won the Indy local and a heat at the All-American Soap Box Derby.

In 1993, my daughter Kelly won the Akron local and placed eighth in the All-American. The trophy is still in the living room. In 1998, Kelly won the NDR (National Derby Rallies) National Championship.

Other favorites memories include being on the *Today* show in 2003 promoting the Derby, being on ESPN, the front page of the *Akron Beacon Journal*, and being inducted into the Derby Hall of Fame the same day in 2006. I was too young for the 25th Derby and my nephew Chris lost in the 50th, but in 2012 my granddaughter, Trinity Kubick, won the 75th Akron local. —*Jeff "Mr. Derby" Iula, co-author with Bill Ignizio of* How I Saw It: My Photographic Memory of the Soap Box Derby

COURTESY CAR DRIVER AT THE DERBY

The Soap Box Derby was always after the Fourth of July, and my husband (James Sorgi) would take a week's vacation to drive a courtesy car for the Soap Box Derby. He did that for about 20 years. He went to a hotel in Akron and stayed there; he didn't even come home. —*Nancy Sorgi*

TROPHY TIME: In Akron, Bill Ford won the 1970 local title that entitled him to compete in the World Championships at the All-American Soap Box Derby.

DATES IN ALL-AMERICAN SOAP BOX DERBY HISTORY

- 1934: First All-American Soap Box Derby is held in Dayton

- 1935: The event moves to Akron

- 1971: Girls compete in the derby for the first time

- 1975: The first girl wins the All-American Soap Box Derby (11-year-old Karren Stead of Pennsylvania)

AUTOCROSS IN THE RTA LOT

I remember Autocross in the RTA lot. Our BMW car club and members of the Porsche and Mercedes-Benz car clubs were able to use the parking lot on weekends to put on a fun driving skills event in 1990. We set up a challenging course using traffic cones, but these are not the kind of construction pylons you want to avoid. Your skill test in this single-car timed event is to aim for the cones to cut the course, coming as close as possible. A cone knocked down or pushed out of its chalk-mark box costs you a second or two. A clean run with no cones disturbed counts toward your best timed run. It was hard to get a fastest time with cones completely unscathed. The event would end with bragging rights for the winners, since different classes of vehicles competed for multiple awards. There was an overall fastest-time winner, too.

Some highly modified cars were entered and brought to the lot on trailers, but most of us just changed tires for our competition setup.

—*Terry Morgan*

STOCK CAR RACES

When I was six years old in the 1960s, my dad was the manager and announcer at Painesville Speedway. Our family did a lot of things together, and going to the stock car racetrack was no different. I felt very out of place there. The only comfort was hearing my father's voice from the announcer's booth, knowing he was up there watching over me.

There were a few perks to being a manager's kid: We got to go into the pits and onto the racetrack, and the drivers and pit crews were always very nice to us. The best summer day I had there was when our whole family sat on top of a recently smashed-up stock car on the track. We all had our picture taken together.

For me, the best part of going to the speedway was when we would pile into the car and drive home to Lakewood. It was well past my bedtime as we drove home, and because I was the smallest, I got to sleep on the back window ledge of the car while my brother and sister sprawled out, sleeping on the back seat. This was pre-seatbelt days. It's the only time I didn't have to ride in the middle of the back seat with the hump on the floor.

—*Laurie Ghetia-Orr*

A SMASHING GOOD TIME: In 1961, Painesville Speedway was one of several places where locals could watch car races.

WHAT'S THE SPEEDWAY LIMIT HERE? You got tickets if you watched people driving fast at Painesville Speedway, 1961.

SUMMER GO-KART RACING

I used to hang out at Dan's Pure Oil located in the Cedar-Fairmount shopping district in Cleveland Heights, where Fifth Third Bank is now. One day, I discovered a Royal Norseman go-kart in the basement that Dan Gordon was trying to sell for the owner. I sang the blues to my parents about how life without a Royal Norseman go-kart would be difficult at best. Much to my amazement, they bought it for me. After tearing up the turf in our yard with four-wheel drifts, trying to emulate the great racer Stirling Moss, I decided to rev up my racing repertoire.

TURNING KART WHEELS:
Go-karts were all the rage in 1963.

I built a series of ramps in the back-yard, within a circular course. Speeding around the course, I went airborne every time I hit a ramp. Then, I decided to build a fire just off the high end of one of the ramps. I accelerated around the course, and when I hit the ramp, I was launched over and through the fire.

Unfortunately, I did not notice that repeated trips up the ramp had loosened its underpinnings. Around the course I came, the neighbor kids green with envy. I hit the ramp and it folded under me. My triumphant grin turned into screams as the forward momentum of the go-kart caused it to slalom through the blazing logs. To my horror and extreme discomfort, I scooped up a lapful of fire. Fortunately, jeans were really tough in those days.

My neighbor Ray also had a go-kart, but his machine sat up higher off the ground like a golf cart. One day, I went over to his house to see if he wanted to race together and he came around a blind corner of his driveway and accidentally hit me. The kart hit my ankles and shot me into the air. When I came down, I was spread-eagled over the steering wheel and Ray's body. I also had my arm over his shoulder and draped across the spark plug! He couldn't see, because I was draped across him and we were both con-vulsing like biology-class frogs with the 20,000 volts from the kart's spark plug going through my body into his. I finally got knocked off the spark plug when Ray, blind and shocked, crashed through a neighbor's six-foot hedge. Neither of us told our parents. Our racing days would have been over.

—Stephen Bellamy

Motorized races weren't the only kind. Clevelanders remember everything from bicycles to horses. In fact, outings to Thistledown and Northfield Park made for great summer entertainment.

CYCLING IN THE NORTH COAST HARBOR NCC TRIATHLON, 1988

I didn't do the whole thing. We were a relay team from Lubrizol, and I did the cycling part. The greatest feeling was heading out of downtown all the way to a turn-point in Shaker Heights because the traffic was stopped at all the intersections. I felt important; the traffic cops were working for my benefit. —*Terry Morgan*

THISTLEDOWN MEMORIES

My parents loved horse racing. They started taking me to the track in the 1960s when I was really young. During the summer we went more often. Some weekends we stayed overnight at the Howard Johnson Motor Lodge next to Thistledown. It was so close I could hear them calling the races from the swimming pool. We'd get up early and go to Thistledown, where they only ran day races, and play the thoroughbred horses. We'd leave, eat dinner at the Northfield Inn, and then go to the Northfield track, where they only had night racing, and play the Standardbred horses and harness horses that are trotters and pacers.

You'd place your bet at the window and hope for a winner. There were good days and bad days, but we just went for the enjoyment of watching the horses. Both tracks had a clubhouse where you could eat—the view of the track was great, with all of those windows. The Ohio Derby is held once a year at Thistledown. It used to be on Father's Day. It is the biggest race in Ohio and has the richest purse. I went to the track as often as I could when I got older. I'd ride there with my parents, drive out with friends, or take the Rapid to Warrensville, and then take a bus or walk to Thistledown to play the horses. —*Patrick Flynn*

OFF TO THE RACES: The Ohio Derby was just one of the Thistledown events in the summer of 1981.

"You'd place your bet at the window and hope for a winner."

SUMMER JOB AT THISTLEDOWN'S VALET LOT

It was a cool job, working at Thistledown. I probably lost more in gambling than I made in tips. It was cool, because anybody who was anybody who came to the racetrack, came through the valet lot. That was prestige, so there were some really, really nice cars you got to drive. Sometimes you'd get really big tips. Celebrities would come through, and because I was low man on the totem pole I wasn't allowed to drive the celebrities' cars. It was cool; I was among a lot of muckety-mucks.

Think about this: I was a kid, 16, 17, and 18 and I loved gambling back in those days. I liked the racetrack. We got paid pretty well, and we got tips and were working outside. The majority of the work was at the beginning of the race day, which is noon to one o'clock, and at the end of the day, from five to six. So you had your evenings. You could wake up late, so it was a great job. It was low pressure; I never got into an accident. I learned how to drive a stick, and I learned on a "three on the tree" (three on the column) there, which was kind of cool. You had a whole host of characters. I mean, you had some of the trainers, who would normally go through the trainer way, but would come through the valet way if they were bringing somebody else. There were the jockeys, lawyers, and then you'd have the gamblers and the pimps. It was a great mix. Racetracks are great for someone like me. I rarely go now. It has completely changed.

I loved horses. —*Steve Presser*

STEERING COMMITTEE: When one kid in the neighborhood got a cool car, everybody wanted a turn at the wheel.

THISTLEDOWN
JOCKEY CLUB

Traditionally OHIO'S Finest

1955 *Meeting*
May 26th thru July 15th

Price Fifteen Cents

COLORS OF SUMMERS PAST: Thistledown race track in North Randall has been around since 1925.

SHOWING THE FLAG: Locals turned out for Fourth of July festivities at local parks.

SUMMER IN THE CITY

Downtown of Renown

Trips downtown were a summertime adventure offering the chance to ride streetcars or the Rapid, cruise the department stores, and float along the sidewalks to window-shop and take advantage of all that downtown had to offer. That might include having lunch, stopping for a Frosty Malt in Higbee's basement, visiting the Cleveland Public Library or the Terminal Tower observation deck, or even seeing a movie.

DOWNTOWN TREATS

During the summers, once a week my grandmother would meet my Aunt Louise downtown. My aunt lived on the west side. My grandmother and I would get on the Windermere Rapid and meet my aunt downtown for lunch at the Higbee's Silver Grille, Halle's Geranium Room, Woolworth's, Kresge's, or Mills Cafeteria. Sometimes when it was Ladies' Day they would see a movie, too. We went to the Hippodrome. One time, they thought they were going to see *Lady L* with Sophia Loren, and what was actually playing that day was a Hell's Angels movie. They both fell asleep, but I was there, watching. When they woke up, they realized this wasn't *Lady L*! Afterward, they took me to get a Frosty and a treat at Hough Bakery. I loved the blondies, and the Miamis at Hough Bakery, those glazed twisty doughnuts that were so wonderful, and their white cake. —*Larry Fox*

COOL LUNCH SPOT: Halle's Geranium Room was in full flower in 1964.

HOUGH STUFF: No matter what you brought to the picnic, breads, and pastries from Hough Bakeries were always people-pleasers.

RIDE TO THE TRIBE:
In 1962, you could take this bus to the Cleveland Municipal Stadium box office.

(left)

MAY'S IN SUMMER:
The May Company downtown.

(right)

JUNE AT HIGBEE'S:
Summer shoppers browse downtown in 1964.

SUMMER TRIPS DOWNTOWN, CIRCA 1964

A highlight for me, one of my favorite things for years, was a trip downtown via the Rapid to the Terminal Tower, where I would zip up to the top and enjoy the observation deck. I had never been in a large city before, so I would take my time looking around and seeing the entire city laid out. I was particularly taken aback by the large brown stain that exited the mouth of the Cuyahoga and stained what was to the west, a perfectly blue lake, into the most awful colors you could see, and to the east as far as the eye could go.

And then I would come back down from the observation deck and go over to the Cleveland Public Library, the main branch downtown, and I would always try to go via the Old Arcade. I thought that, architecturally, it was one of the most fascinating buildings I had ever seen. To a boy from the country, this was a big deal. I had most recently lived in rural Maryland, where my dad worked for the government doing aerospace stuff. —*Sam Bell*

EUCLID AVENUE IN THE SUMMER

One of my summer memories is going downtown, back in the day when Stouffer's Restaurants littered Euclid Avenue and there were Bonwit Teller and Milgrim's uptown, east of Halle's. I would meet my grandmother. She always parked at 17th and Euclid in the Hanna parking lot. We met at Stouffer's, had lunch, and then went shopping. Sometimes I took the bus downtown with my friend on the weekends, and we would pretty much traverse all of Euclid Avenue because, heaven forbid, we would see something at Higbee's and she would say, "I'm going to buy this, but not until we go down to Halle's." That was maybe 14 blocks away, and she wanted to make sure there was nothing there that was any better. —*Maribeth Katt*

WE WAIT ALL YEAR FOR SUMMER, SO WE MIGHT AS WELL MAKE THE BEST OF IT

For the working stiff, there is no summer—at least not the long stretches of school-free bliss we all remember from childhood. My first summer working downtown, I had no vacation days, and summer slipped away while I sat at a green metal desk pounding a manual typewriter.

The work was routine, which freed me up mentally to feel sorry for myself. One Monday morning, when a co-worker burst into tears because it had rained all weekend for three weekends in a row, I realized I had better get a grip. So I decided to appreciate the summer I did have. I enjoyed the RTA Rapid ride downtown, so grim in the winter, but in the summer overgrown with honeysuckle and Queen Anne's lace. I savored my lunch hours outside—cooling my feet in the Fountain of Eternal Life and enjoying the festive crowds of women dressed in white who descended on Cleveland every summer for church conventions. I browsed the fiction stacks in the magnificent Cleveland Public Library and ate my lunch solo with dozens of other introverts in the Eastman Reading Garden. I drifted around in the air-conditioned shopper's heaven that was Higbee's department store, and I frequented a vintage jewelry shop on the second level of the Old Arcade. Sometimes I just walked all the way down the Mall to the overlook and took in Lake Erie. It was different every day, but always beautiful. Blue sky, blue lake, white sailboats— a wonderful place to be in the summer.

—*Meredith Holmes*

(left)
SUMMER SHOPPERS: Downtown drew people to shop at department stores such as Higbee's, Halle's, and The May Company.

(right)
SQUARE DEAL: The Cleveland Orchestra plays on Public Square, July 4, 1990.

FUN IN THE FLATS: An art fair in 1977 (above) and a vibrant scene in 1988 (left).

"Blue sky, blue lake, white sailboats —a wonderful place to be in the summer."

Community Activities

East side or west side, local celebrations were always memories in the making. The character of our communities has contributed to the fond childhood memories of special events held close to home. Some events centered around food—perhaps ribs or ethnic favorites at the All Nations Festival—while others focused on seasonal holidays such as Memorial Day, July Fourth, and Labor Day. You might recall Concerts on the Mall, the Party in the Park series, or Parties in the Flats, the BP Riverfest, the Coventry Street Fair, Hessler Street Fair, Feast of the Assumption and other church festivals around town.

MEAT AND GREET: Cleveland Mayor Ralph Perk stops to talk to participants at one of the food tables during the 1973 All Nations Festival.

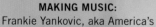

MAKING MUSIC: Frankie Yankovic, aka America's Polka King, plays at the 1976 All Nations Festival in Cleveland.

ROCKY RIVER DAYS

Rocky River Days were held at Rocky River Park in the '60s. There was a whole host of games for kids of all ages to participate in: sack races, water balloon tosses, candy runs, etc. There were other activities throughout the park, such as Captain Penny handing out free Popsicles, bands playing in the grandstand, bicycle decorating contests, and fireworks at the end of the day. It was always a great time you looked forward to every year, and reminisced about years past. —*Rhea Wightman*

COVENTRY STREET FAIR IN THE '70S, CLEVELAND HEIGHTS

I was on the committee that planned the first Coventry Street Fair: Interminable meetings in which very few things ever got decided, but we somehow ended up putting on a very fun event that has continued ever since.
—*Kathleen Cerveny*

FEAST OF THE ASSUMPTION, LITTLE ITALY

I've been going to "The Feast" every year for more than 60 years. The big day is August 15th, and The Feast usually runs for four days. It has been the highlight of the summer when friends meet and get to see each other, whether they are still living here in Little Italy or have moved away and come back to celebrate. For about the past 15 years, I have been making authentic costumes from the different regions and cities in Italy, and they are worn in the procession. There are open houses where families get together and enjoy the meals, and so much more. —*Barbara Mongelluzzi*

FOOD AT THE FEAST

We would walk from Cleveland Heights, down Kenilworth Road, Edgehill Road and then Murray Hill to attend the Little Italy festival. Great food and great fun. —*Sally Slater Wilson*

THE CLEVELAND AIR SHOW ON LABOR DAY WEEKEND

One thing I looked forward to every year was the Air Show, with the Navy's Blue Angels and all the aircraft flying by overhead. I was always into aircraft, and made model airplanes as a kid. —*Steve Horniak*

CHURCH CARNIVAL IN AVON LAKE

I remember waiting for the St Joseph's Summer Carnival in Avon Lake in August. It was the last big event of the summer before going back to school. It was great to just hang out with no cares in the world, with friends in that environment. A couple of Sno Cones and cotton candy made for a good day at the carnival. I also remember hanging out with the "carny" guys. That was different. Now that I think about it, summer was a time that I was doing stuff I had no business doing. —*Paul Negulescu*

Weather—You Like it, or Not

Amid the beautiful summer days, we've had some extremes—unseasonably chilly weather as well as scorchers. Temperatures reached 101°F on September 1, 1953, in an era before air conditioners at home were common.

Check out these Cleveland temperatures during some of the summer holidays in years past.

MEMORIAL DAY

55°F in 1984
90°F in 1988

JULY FOURTH

66°F high in 1961 and 1967
68°F high in 1960
69°F high in 1972 and 1978
94°F high in 1974
96°F high in 1955
98°F high in 1949

LABOR DAY

60°F high in 1958
93°F high in 1973
98°F high in 1954

(left)
LOOK UP: The National Air Races, first held in Cleveland in 1929, evolved into the Cleveland National Air Show in 1964.

(right)
COVENTRY STREET FAIR, 1981: This Cleveland Heights tradition started in the mid-1970s.

Hot Town, Summer in the '60s

If you were around in the 1960s, you might remember some of these milestone events. Unless you were too busy watching Ghoulardi on WJW-TV, Channel 8, that is.

1961: The Great Lakes Shakespeare Festival is founded; its first performance ("As You Like It") opens at the festival's home in the Lakewood Civic Auditorium the following summer, on July 11, 1962.

1962: Cuyahoga County joins the fight against polio with a voluntary mass immunization program—Sabin Oral Sundays—extending from May to July. Sabin Oral Polio Vaccine was administered on sugar cubes distributed at more than 90 locations, primarily schools, in Greater Cleveland.

1963: Daily transportation service from Public Square to Euclid Beach Park ends.

1964: The Davis Cup final is played in Cleveland Heights at Roxboro Junior High School's 7,500-seat stadium.

1965: Jungle Larry's African Safari opens at Cedar Point.

1966: The Beatles' WIXY-sponsored concert comes to Cleveland Stadium on August 14.

1967: Groundbreaking ceremonies for Blossom Music Center take place on July 2, 1967.

1968: Judy Collins, The Association, Herb Alpert, Ravi Shankar, The Young Americans, Harry Belafonte and Louis Armstrong were on the 1968 Jazz-Folk schedule at Blossom Music Center.

1969: On September 28, 1969, Euclid Beach Park closes.

CROWD PARTICIPATION: An impressive crowd gathered for the procession that began at Holy Rosary Church in Little Italy during the Feast of the Assumption in 1962.

WINNING TOSS AT THE LORAIN AVENUE STREET FESTIVAL

I must have been about 10 or 11. We lived on West 101st Street off of Lorain, and there was a street fair that shut Lorain Avenue down, from just past our street to about 98th Street (at least I think it went down that far).

It was a different time then, so my parents allowed me to go to this street fair with my friend. I played the game where you toss a ping pong ball and hope it lands in a fish bowl with a goldfish in it. Some of the bowls were just filled with water. As I think about it now, the game was run by what I thought at the time was a grungy old man who was kind of scary. The games were set up on the sidewalk with the operator sitting in a chair in the small recessed doorways of the businesses along Lorain Avenue.

I threw that ping-pong ball and watched it bounce on the rim of about five fishbowls. Then, to my extreme delight, it landed in a fishbowl with a fish. I was so excited I screamed, jumped up and down and took my prize with pride. I felt like I had just won the lottery.

I took that five-minute walk home like a victory lap smiling from ear to ear. My goldfish, named Goldie, didn't live all that long. However, it began a chain of events that led me to have several other fish, like the ones with the eyes that bulge, a few beta fish, and, finally, an aquarium that my dad set up in the living room. I'd help him pick the fish and feed them. Once, after we cleaned the tank, one of the fish actually jumped out of an open door flap of the tank.

To this day, I remember the feeling of winning that goldfish that started my interest in marine life. —*Nikole Ortiz*

THE FOOLS FAIR AT LAKE ERIE COLLEGE IN PAINESVILLE

Lake Erie College had what they called The Fools Fair for several years, and that is where they had the Society for Creative Anachronism group perform. Those guys were really zealous about what they did. There were so into it. I remember the costumes being pretty heavy, and the armor. It was summer, and really hot. The women wore long gowns, probably really heavy, and flower wreaths in their hair. My recollection is that they had armor and weapons. They roasted a pig, and it was never done. I liked it because everybody was there from my college, hanging out on the lawn. —*Maribeth Katt*

Lots of Balloons

On September 27, 1986, nearly 1.5 million balloons were released in Cleveland's Public Square. The United Way-sponsored fundraiser BalloonFest '86 is said to have set a Guinness World Record for being the largest mass balloon release. Here's a behind-the-scenes peek at the people who inflated all those balloons.

BALLOON BUILDING

The quadrant of Public Square closest to Higbee's was surrounded by a rectangle of scaffolding approximately two stories tall. This scaffolding had a "skin" applied of woven mesh material to keep the inflated balloons corralled until they were ready to be released. The roof over the scaffold was also composed of suspended mesh. On command, larger balloons tugging on the outside of the mesh would help lift the mesh roof away, thus allowing the balloons to escape.

I have pictures of the event in which you can see the height of the scaffolding in relation to the Higbee's sign and the huge bulging balloon mass straining against the woven mesh roof.

Hundreds of students were bused in to inflate balloons as they sat at tables with helium nozzles. The task was simple: Pull the open end of the balloon over the nozzle. Open the valve to inflate the balloon, remove it carefully, tie a knot in the balloon, and release it to rise to the roof.

—*Stephen Bellamy*

EXCITEMENT IN THE AIR: Balloonfest '86, sponsored by United Way in September, was the largest balloon release on record: 1,429,643.

WHAT'S UP WITH BALLOONFEST? In 1986, students inflated balloons to get ready for the balloon release event.

TOTALLY CUBULAR: SABIN ORAL SUNDAYS, 1962

During the summer of 1962, when Cleveland launched a program designed to wipe out polio in Cuyahoga County, all the neighborhoods in the city got into the act. The Cleveland Academy of Medicine Public Health Committee, chaired by Dr. Howard H. Hopwood, Jr., implemented the SOS, or Sabin Oral Sundays, that took place over a six-week period. Thanks to this program of the Cleveland Academy of Medicine, an estimated 90 percent of Clevelanders took the oral polio vaccine. The vaccine itself was developed by Dr. Albert B. Sabin, and it was administered by applying a drop of the vaccine to a sugar cube that was then eaten.

The plan was a voluntary effort modeled on a program in Phoenix, Ariz. The Cleveland program involved three times as many people and was the largest of its kind in the United States, with approximately 90 vaccination centers set up at area schools, all within walking distance of participating Cuyahoga County residents.

July Fourth Memories

Whether you celebrated on your own street or went to any of the many fireworks displays around town, July Fourth was, and is, a high point of summer.

FESTIVAL OF FREEDOM

Nothing says summer like fireworks on the Fourth of July, and there was nothing quite like the fireworks at Edgewater Park—the Festival of Freedom. It may not have been the best fireworks show in town, but it was always the best spectacle.

From Edgewater Park, you could see a fantastic view of the Cleveland skyline and the fireworks show at Lakewood Park, which usually ended before the Cleveland show started.

More than 100,000 people would jam onto the 900-foot beach and all of the surrounding hills in the 130-acre park to watch the 20-minute sky show.

Beach blankets and portable barbecues marked everyone's territory. Picnic tables packed with families looked like lifeboats in this sea of every-color faces. It wasn't just your neighbors and friends who were there, it was everyone from the entire city and surrounding suburbs and their neighbors and friends who were there with you.

The crowds got so large, the city had to close the Shoreway so that people could park their cars on the roadway and walk into and out of the park without having to worry about the speeding traffic.

Most of the crowd got there early and stayed all day so they could enjoy the water and lounge on the beach and eat and drink and get the best viewing spots.

There was live music and the local radio stations would broadcast live from the beach all day long, and then play music to accompany the fireworks show.

FAMILY FUN BLANKETS THE PARK: The 1970 Festival of Freedom at Edgewater Park.

(continued)

Registration forms were mailed to Clevelanders at home, and forms were also available in local newspapers. Area residents were asked to fill out the forms and bring them to the closest immunization site. This voluntary mass immunization program was free, although contributions were suggested (25 cents). During that summer, 10,000 volunteers administered vaccines to more than 800,000 (by some estimates more than a million) residents of Cuyahoga County. Up to $1 million in time and materials was donated to implement the program, which included efforts by United Appeal public relations man Charles Nekvasil, the McCann-Marschalk advertising agency with members of the Cleveland graphic arts community, and the Academy of Medicine, Cleveland.

On the designated Sundays, sugar cube vaccinations proceeded at a rate of 1,000 people an hour for eight hours at each of the immunization centers. The total estimated cost of the program: $500,000. It was an all-volunteer program, with the only paid employee being one full-time secretary. Each site was staffed by 10 nurses, 15 Boy Scouts, three Girl Scouts, 12 P.T.A. members, and volunteers from other groups. The vaccines were distributed on May 27, June 3, June 24, July 1, July 22, and July 29.

If you got there at dusk, you were greeted by the smells of barbecuing chicken and ribs and hamburgers combined with the fishy beach and suntan lotion and marijuana. The sounds of live music, live radio broadcasts and thousands of radios tuned to different stations mingled with the sounds of laughter and screaming, English and Spanish, and the patter of vendors. You could barely hear the person standing next to you. Something good or bad could happen at any moment. It was alive. It was electric. It was dangerous. It was wonderful. —*Tom Papadimoulis*

Get Ready for the Fireworks

EDGEWATER PARK FIREWORKS ON JULY FOURTH

It was pretty cool—you could sit on the hill and it was just peppered with people. It was kind of interesting looking out at the lake. You would see the reflection of fireworks on the lake. One time, I remember seeing the moon on the lake and the fireworks, and thinking, "This is pretty spectacular, with a panoramic view of Winton Place on the left, downtown Cleveland on the right, and the lake in front of me." The setting was so unique. —*Steve Horniak*

GEAUGA LAKE FIREWORKS

On July Fourth every year, Geauga Lake put on a spectacular fireworks display. That was a treat, a highlight of the summer at the cottage. We would all march up on the evening of July Fourth, sit on the railroad tracks with a spectacular view of the park and the lake, and enjoy this great fireworks show. —*Dennis Gaughan*

Summer in the '70s

It was the disco era when the film *Saturday Night Fever* starring John Travolta was released (1977), the decade that the Richfield Coliseum opened (1974), and the Sony Walkman arrived on the scene (1979). It was also during the '70s that the following events took place in Northeast Ohio. If you remember any of these summer happenings, there's also a chance that you've seen a leisure suit first-hand.

- SeaWorld of Ohio opens in Aurora (1970)

- Coventry Street Fair launches in Cleveland Heights (1974)

- The Pink Floyd Concert at the World Series of Rock in Cleveland Municipal Stadium draws 83,000. Tickets were $10 in advance (June 25, 1977)

- More than 82,000 fans head to The Rolling Stones concert at Cleveland Municipal Stadium (July 1, 1978)

- Clevelanders put on hard hats for Skylab parties and await the return of the Skylab U.S. space station to earth (July 11, 1979)

FIREWORKS AT LAKEWOOD PARK

I remember one year, when I was older, I was at a party on St. Charles Avenue. I had to work nights, so I was just leaving the party on July Fourth, walking back to my car, and they started shooting off the fireworks. I remember thinking, "That's weird. They're starting with the grand finale." They had all gone off at once. —*Dave Davis*

AND ALL OF A SUDDEN . . .

One year, all the fireworks went off at one time in Lakewood Park. That was incredible! It was a mishap, but pretty amazing. —*Steve Horniak*

FIREWORKS AT MUNICIPAL STADIUM

My earliest memory of going to see fireworks was up at Berea quarry. And of course, I was desperate to see fireworks at the old stadium. That was when the old scoreboard was in full force. Whenever anyone hit a home run, the horns would swing out from the side and torches would go off from the top and searchlights would swing around and then—boom!—the fireworks. —*Joe Gunderman*

FIREWORKS, UP CLOSE AND PERSONAL

My wife is from the suburbs and had never seen anything like West 76th Street or the Festival of Freedom. She was used to more tame and homogenized events. She was equally terrified and excited by it.

The fireworks were always spectacular. It always felt like we were right in the middle of every burst of fiery color, surrounded by the crackle, sizzle, and boom of every round that was launched into the night sky, but we never got there early enough to stake out a prime spot.

What would it be like if we got really close to the launch site?

One year, we arrived early and found a spot near the rocky breakwall at the end of the beach. There weren't many people there yet. We thought it would be the perfect spot, and it was, until the wind shifted.

For a while, we were right in the center of every beautiful explosion of color. Each one expanded in the sky and threatened to swallow us whole as it grew and grew and rushed toward us. It was everything we thought it would be. Even in a crowd this big, we were able to shut out all of the ooohs and aaahs except our own. It felt intimate and romantic. And then we noticed the sparks and fiery debris that were suddenly raining down on us.

The wind had shifted and instead of sending the remains of the spent rounds out to the lake, the wind was sending them right at us.

We were in the middle of it all, all right. Fire and ash rained down on us from every direction. The grand finale only made matters worse when every last bomb was shot into the air at once for a deafening, blinding show of sound and color. We dodged burning cardboard chunks and incinerated metal fragments and coughed our way through the cloud of sulfur smoke that was now right on top of us. No matter where we ran for cover, the exploded leftovers followed us. We had to avoid them, as well as all of the other people who had thought it would be a good idea to find a spot closer to the fireworks.

It was like a scene out of a Japanese monster movie. I don't ever remember being quite that scared or laughing quite that hard. We could be burned alive or trampled to death, but it didn't matter. We were having a great time.

It was the best fireworks show we had ever seen. I don't think we'll ever forget the sights and sounds and smells.

We still talk about the Festival of Freedom today—every Fourth of July, as we watch our safe suburban fireworks celebrations—far from the danger and the excitement of that night at Edgewater Park. —*Tom Papadimoulis*

"*It was like a scene out of a Japanese monster movie.*"

HIGH AND MIGHTY: Festival of Freedom fireworks over Cleveland Municipal Stadium in 1976.

FREE TO BE: One of many memorable Festivals of Freedom held at Edgewater Park.

AN ERIE FEELING: Edgewater Park was the scene of this music festival in 1972.

HAVING A BALL IN CLEVELAND

The Season of Sports

We enjoyed a thriving all-around sports culture in Cleveland, including Major League Baseball, softball, golf, and tennis. In the past, local kids attended their first Cleveland Indians baseball games at League Park at East 66th and Lexington, while others fondly recall Cleveland Municipal Stadium on the lakefront. When Municipal Stadium opened in 1931, it seated 78,189 and was said to be the world's largest outdoor arena. A milestone event for younger fans was the opening of Jacobs Field (now Progressive Field) on Ontario Street, with its 43,345 seating capacity, in 1994.

A GAME TO REMEMBER, 1954

In 1954 when I was seven, my father, Peter Bellamy, was a reporter for the *Cleveland News*. He got press tickets for a Cleveland Indians baseball game and for my birthday, he took me and my older sister to a game at Cleveland Municipal Stadium.

My father deftly avoided the large crowds generated by a season that was capped by the Indians becoming the American League champions. He led us upstairs to the Wigwam, a private restaurant for sportswriters and Indians officials. During our lunch, sportswriters stopped by to greet my father. I realized we were backstage at the ballpark, and I was really impressed.

STAR SPANGLED OPENING OF JACOBS FIELD: The National Anthem was provided by The Cleveland Orchestra and Chorus.

The New Base Ball Park, Cleveland, Ohio.

BASEBALL MILESTONES AT LEAGUE PARK

- 1920, First World Series grand slam and the First World series triple play
- 1929, Babe Ruth's 500th home run
- 1936, Bob Feller's first major-league start as a pitcher
- 1945, Home of the Negro World Series champs, the Cleveland Buckeyes

HEAR HERE: In 1954, Cleveland Indians fans listened to games on the radio with sportscaster Jimmy Dudley and watched Channel 8 to see on-the-road games.

A man stopped by our table and asked, "Hey, Pete, are these your kids?" I had never met him, but I recognized the voice of Jimmy Dudley, the famous play-by-play announcer for the Indians. Wow! This was Jimmy Dudley, the man I'd heard over the radio countless times saying, "The string is out," or, "Brought to you by Kahn's all-meat wieners—the wiener the world awaited." Many people probably remember his trademark sign off, "Lots of good luck, ya hear?"

Walking to our seats that day, I was enchanted by the large crowd, the immensity of the stadium, and the smells of hot dogs, popcorn, and green grass. Jimmy Dudley walked by our seats on his way to his announcer's position that was set off from the crowd only by pipe railings. When he saw us, he stopped and asked if I wanted to sit next to him as he did the play-by-play. I jumped up.

The eyes of the crowd were on Jimmy Dudley in the press box before the game began. Many times I had heard him speak of a foul ball that had just missed him as it caromed off the Coke machine in the press box—and there it was, in all its battered glory.

During the best baseball game of my life, I got to see my favorite player, outfielder Larry Doby, make a seemingly impossible catch as he jumped and bent his back over the outfield fence to corral a ball. I later grabbed a foul ball on the bounce, and my father got the whole team to autograph it. That ball would be worth a lot today. I wonder where it is. —*Stephen Bellamy*

PLAY BALL! A memorable Cleveland Indians game, July 1954.

MEMORABLE GAMES IN 1954 AND 1955

The Cleveland Indians won the American League pennant in 1954, winning a record 111 games. My dad took me to the final home game of the season, and I fell in love with the entire experience. The next two summers, when I was 12 and 13 years old, I attended more than 30 games each year. I took the bus from my home on West 97th Street and arrived at Cleveland Municipal Stadium at 11 a.m. to watch batting practice. After the games, I stayed to get autographs and take photos of the players. I still have my autograph book and autographed photos. One special day was a doubleheader on May 1, 1955, when Bob Feller pitched his twelfth one-hitter, and in the second game, rookie Herb Score struck out 16 batters. My favorite player was the Indians' catcher, Jim Hegan, who caught many of Feller's games over the years. —*Lois Gollwitzer Dixon*

WHICH INDIANS?

The summer I turned five, my dad said we were going downtown to see the Indians. I thought he meant Native American Indians. When I learned he meant baseball Indians I was both disappointed and excited. Before the game, my Dad took my sister—who had won the tickets from the Cleveland Press for being a straight-A student at St. Mary's grade school in Bedford—and me to the observation deck of the Terminal Tower. I had never been that high up and the view was magical; so were the sights I saw for the first time when we claimed our seats at the old Municipal Stadium. I remember being awestruck by the bright green, expansive outfield; the muted beige, well-groomed infield; and the perfectly straight, bright white baselines. That day I became hooked on baseball and baseball Indians. —*Joe Jancsurak*

CLEVELAND MUNICIPAL STADIUM, 1976

I attended many Indians games, and was a big fan of the Tribe. I took pride in watching games as a bleacher bum in the Cheap Seats Elite. But when the opportunity presented itself to be on the field with a press pass from my brother, I jumped at the chance. In order to go, I needed to call off sick from my job as a nurse at Lakewood Hospital. I was lucky enough to stand next to Rick Manning, whom I'd had a crush on for years, and have our picture taken together. The Shriners were on the field that day for the seventh-inning break, along with the Crazy Cops and their miniature paddy wagon. They picked me up as a fake prisoner, put on plastic handcuffs, and drove me around the stadium field for all to see. As the paddy wagon ride came to an end, the vehicle slowed and I looked up at the crowd in the lower box seats. There were my two nursing supervisors, looking right back at me. It was worth the trouble I got into to have the picture of Rick Manning standing next to me. —*Laurie Ghetia-Orr*

"I was lucky enough to stand next to Rick Manning, whom I'd had a crush on for years."

VIEW OF THE PAST: The Horticultural Gardens were built north of Municipal Stadium for the Great Lakes Exposition, 1936–37.

EVENTFUL DAYS AT THE STADIUM: You never knew what special events and seventh-inning attractions you might encounter at a Cleveland Indians baseball game.

NIFTY FIFTIES: 1950 was the Cleveland Indians' 50th season. That year, they finished fourth in the American League.

FAN FAVORITE: Centerfielder Rick Manning made his major-league debut with the Cleveland Indians in 1975.

CLOSE CALL

We used to go to the Indians games and my uncle had something to do with the grounds crew, so we actually got to sit in the section on the third-base line where they would roll out the tarp.

This was pre-ball boys and they used to tell you, "You can't go on the field." Once, when a ball came down, I reached over—I had my mitt, of course. I got the ball, but as I reached over, I fell onto the field. I thought, "Oh my God, lightning is literally going to strike me. I'm dead. You're not allowed on the field; it's illegal."

I got up and the place was cheering me because I had done a flip-over. I was so nervous I hid. That's the only ball that I got, and I don't consider it to be a ball that was caught at the stadium. But it was great. —*Steve Presser*

LISTENING ON THE RADIO

My mom loved to listen to the Indians on the radio. If it was a really hot day, she would make hot dogs and we would eat in the basement while listening, because it was cooler down there. —*Carol Evans Abel*

People Who Made the Stadium Experience More Memorable

If your memories of Cleveland Municipal Stadium involve scoreboard fireworks when the Cleveland Indians hit a home run, or rallying music played live on the organ, these are some of the folks you can thank.

BACH, BELLS, AND BASEBALL

My dad shared with me his enthusiasm for both classical music and baseball. He saved everything—Cleveland Orchestra programs and Cleveland Indians scorecards, all annotated in his perfect hand-lettering.

In 1993, I combined my passions for performing improvised music and watching baseball. I was certain the phone call was a prank by one of my brother's softball buddies, but it was legit: an invitation to apply for the organist job that last season at Municipal Stadium. (I've since played the last event at the Cleveland Play House Club and several area churches—people are afraid to hire me now!)

I auditioned for Indians' management by playing silent-movie style on their Hammond organ while watching videos of prior games. I landed the job and was interviewed on ESPN. I established the Winchester bell chimes for Albert Belle, "Ain't Misbehavin'" for Kenny Lofton (who stole bases legally), "Maple Leaf Rag" to follow "O Canada," the ominous bass-line from *Jaws* underneath a pre-recorded ad for Sea-World. I got a media nod for "Jingle Bells" when it snowed on an early April game. From the front office's reaction, it seemed Nobel Prize-worthy to do "Hail to the Chief" for an Indians staffer impersonating President Nixon on '70s Nostalgia Day.

It was not a great season for the Tribe, but it was great fun to be the official intruder into the boys' treehouse that was the Scoreboard Room. I'd pray for a rain delay, better yet, a thunderstorm. Then I rocked the house with my haunted house medley: "The Munsters," "Addams Family," Moussorgsky's "Night on Bald Mountain," Bach's D-minor Toccata and Fugue.

My favorite moment of the whole season was "You Can Leave Your Hat On" when Jose Canseco got beaned out in right field and the ball bounced into the stands.

I ate a lot of hot dogs that summer: great Stadium Mustard, great times. My dad loved it. —*Marge Adler*

KNOWING THE SCORE IN '54: A 1954 Cleveland Indians scorecard.

MAY COMPANY DEPARTMENT SCORE: This 1938 World Series scoreboard at The May Company downtown kept everybody up to date on the Yankees and the Cubs.

A BIG HIT: A Cleveland Indians souvenir book, 1954.

LOCAL FIREWORKS CONNECTION

If you remember watching fireworks at Euclid Beach, Geauga Lake or SeaWorld, or waiting for them when the Cleveland Indians hit a home run at the Cleveland Municipal Stadium, you've seen fireworks displays by the American Fireworks Company, based in Hudson. The same goes for fireworks you might have seen at Blossom Music Center, the Feast of the Assumption in Little Italy, or on July Fourth in Cleveland-area communities such as Euclid, Shaker Heights, and Bay Village.

American Fireworks is a family-owned business, started by Vincenzo Sorgi in 1902. Later, his son James and grandson John joined the business. Today, Nancy Sorgi (wife of the late James Sorgi and mother of the late John D. Sorgi) is still active in the company, with her grandsons Roberto and John David now representing the seventh generation of the family to work in pyrotechnics.

Nancy Sorgi started working at the company in 1950, and recalls the years that American Fireworks provided the scoreboard fireworks for Cleveland Municipal Stadium, from the 1950s through the 1970s. She notes that back in the 1950s, her father-in-law was making all the fireworks by hand.

"We were at every Indians game. We had to have a guy on the roof there, because with every home run hit, there were fireworks. The scoreboard fireworks were all aerial, shot salutes for home runs. There were also fireworks shows several times during the summer on Friday nights. We had six or eight men around the field for the shows." *—Nancy Sorgi*

Softball Teams

Companies, neighborhoods, social organizations, and other groups assembled softball teams to play during the summer around Cleveland.

THE CELEBRITY CONNECTION

At General Electric, Nela Park, there was a celebrity softball tournament in July or August. We got to meet Captain Penny, Franz the Toymaker, Woody the Woodsman and Ghoulardi. Every once in awhile, through the years, some of the Cleveland Indians ballplayers would show up, too. Ernie Anderson, Ghoulardi, would show up and he couldn't have been nicer. I have

a picture with my brother holding a little autograph book. We were getting celebrity autographs from everyone that day, but Ernie Anderson was the only one who was actually nice enough to pose for a picture with us.

That's one of our favorite summertime memories—watching my dad play softball, and my grandfather and my dad going to the old stadium on the lake and watching the baseball games in those rickety old seats. —*Larry Fox*

Maybe you recall watching Ghoulardi on WJW-TV, Channel 8 from 1963 to 1966. Many softball fans around town, though, also remember watching his softball team, the Ghoulardi All-Stars. Team members included Chuck "Big Chuck" Schodowski. There were also Ghoulardi All-Stars football, basketball, and hockey teams.

THE GHOULARDI ALL-STARS SOFTBALL TEAM

Ernie Anderson became Ghoulardi in February 1963. Ernie always fancied himself as a jock, so shortly thereafter, he made up the Ghoulardi All-Stars softball team because Captain Penny had one at Channel 5. Ernie got his own team, and he loaded it with some pretty good players. We beat Channel 5. He used to just call me Chuck, but when I played softball I was really good at hitting the ball hard. After I hit four home runs in a game, he started calling me Big Chuck. I'm not all that big; I'm a little over six feet.

Ernie just loved the All-Stars, and we all went out afterwards, had a drink or two, and some camaraderie. Then, all of a sudden, we were going everywhere. It didn't take anything to book a game. All you had to do was talk to Ernie. He would play anybody. One summer, Mid-May to September, we played 56 games. They were all charity events. Think about that—it's about one game every other day. Everybody's wife was mad. —*Chuck "Big Chuck" Schodowski, author of* Big Chuck! My Favorite Stories from 47 Years on Cleveland TV

(left)
DREAM TEAM: The Ghoulardi All-Stars baseball team included celebrities such as Chuck "Big Chuck" Schodowski.

(right)
GHOULARDI FANS: After a Ghoulardi All-Stars appearance in 1965, Ernie "Ghoulardi" Anderson hung around to sign autographs and pose with kids.

'81, ANYONE?
A 1981 souvenir mug.

NO WILD PITCHES AT THE ZOO: Brookside Park, one of the oldest parks in the city, at Fulton Road and Denison Avenue, included a baseball diamond as well as the Cleveland Zoological Park (now the Cleveland Metroparks Zoo).

A LOW SCREAMING LINER

When I was six years old in 1951, I was invited to a Little League game at the baseball park at Monticello and Mayfield. Someone said I could sit by the third-base coach, and I did. About an inning later, a boy hit a low screaming liner that hit me in the head. As I was lying on the grass, someone murmured to me: "Don't worry, old soldiers don't die, they just fade away." I recall being comforted by that statement at the time. But in retrospect, it seems an odd thing to say to a little kid. —*Christine Howey*

PLAY BALL!

While playing in my first Peanut League baseball game, I made it to first base in my first at-bat. I don't recall if I got a hit or walked (this was long before T-ball), but I do remember vividly what took place after. There were two outs, and the coach reminded me to run fast when the batter hit the ball. A couple of pitches later, the batter got a hit and I ran fast, as instructed. When I reached the base, spectators and players alike were laughing. Even the umpire was smiling as he signaled me out. You see, instead of running to second base, I ran across the field and was standing on third base. When I realized my mistake I was crushed. Later that same summer, I was named our team's all-star second baseman.

Play ball! —*Joe Jancsurak*

LITTLE LEAGUE

When I was a real little kid, I played in Middleburg Heights in the City League. I started in T League and moved up through what they called minor leagues, because the major league was Little League. I played a year or two of T League, two years of minors then two years of what is officially Little League, then two years in Class F. I made the All-Star team in the majors the second year.

When I started playing T league I played first base all year long. Somebody even said, "Give somebody else a chance." But I can catch. In T League that was a bit of a premium. —*Joe Gunderman*

SOFTBALL IN LAKEWOOD

When I was older I played softball. We got free T-shirts donated by a local business. Two that I remember are Jackshaw Pontiac and George J. Usher. After softball, it was once again back to the pool. —*Helen Wirt*

RANEY TIRE AT STATE ROAD PARK, 1977

The first Cleveland sports team I rooted for wasn't the Indians or the Browns. It was Raney Tire, a sponsored women's softball team that played at State Road Park in Parma. I had gone to the park one evening with a friend just to kill some time. I know it was 1977 because we were trying to absorb the news that Elvis had just died. All the diamonds were busy—men's and women's teams, slow-pitch and fast-pitch. Fierce games were being played all around.

We wandered over to a field where a large crowd was cheering for a women's team. The team at bat was Raney Tire, and they were terrific. We didn't know then that they had been runners-up in the 1970 Amateur Softball Association of America's national championship. All we knew was it was great to watch women play so hard to win—leaping up to catch fly balls, slugging the ball with all their might, and running full-tilt around the bases. That was the year I discovered there is no better place to be on a summer evening than on a hard wooden seat in the grandstand among the players' most rabid fans—their friends, co-workers, and families. That was the year I became a baseball fan. —*Meredith Holmes*

BASEBALL DATES YOU MIGHT REMEMBER

- 1948: Cleveland Indians win the World Series championship
- 1954: Cleveland Indians set a winning percentage of .721 for the season, still an American League record
- 1964: League Park bleachers are demolished
- 1994: Jacobs Field opens on April 4

SOUVENIRS OF YESTERYEAR: A baseball cap went for a dollar in 1954.

"After softball, it was once again back to the pool."

Getting Good Seats

One way Cleveland students got to Municipal Stadium was by getting the Straight A tickets offered by the Cleveland Press.

THE "A" LIST

The *Cleveland Press*, one of Cleveland's two daily newspapers, ran a promotion in the 1960s to reward schoolchildren for getting straight A's. For every subject in which the student earned straight A's, the Press would award a pair of reserved-seat tickets to an Indians game at Cleveland Municipal Stadium.

For me, A's were very few and far between—let alone straight A's. But, fortunately, I have four very smart sisters, and all of them usually earned straight A's in more than one subject. None of my sisters were big baseball fans, so they'd go to maybe a game a year, and I became the happy recipient of most of the unused tickets. Times were different then, and although we were only about 13, a friend and I would often hop on a #39 CTS bus for the short trip from Euclid to downtown Cleveland.

The stadium was big and dark, and sounds echoed through its concourses. But what I remember most about the stadium are the

REMEMBERING STATE ROAD PARK IN PARMA

I have five kids and when they were little, we lived in Parma for eight years. I was so busy then, working with Ernie (Ernie "Ghoulardi" Anderson) and Hoolie (Bob "Hoolihan the Weatherman" Wells) doing the show. I used to love to come home and throw a football around in the park with my kids and the dog. We lived right across the street from State Road Park with the ball diamonds. Those are probably the nicest summer memories I have. I just loved that part of living in Parma. Now, that's gone—everyone sits in front of the computer. —*Chuck "Big Chuck" Schodowski, author of* Big Chuck! My Favorite Stories from 47 Years on Cleveland TV

SOFTBALL UNDER THE LIGHTS

I remember playing organized baseball and also pick-up games, including playing on the fields where the Lakewood Post Office is now, where the Giant Eagle is now at Detroit and Bunts, and at Harding and Emerson junior high schools. All the games were played during the day, and high school and college kids were the umpires. Mostly, mothers managed the teams. I also played lots of pick-up games on school grounds. My wife and I both remember the men's adult softball games at Harding under the lights. We would go watch them as a family, and I remember a candy store across the street. I was a ball boy for my older brother's team. —*Karl Riccardi*

Other Greater Clevelanders were out there creating summer golf and tennis memories.

TENNIS IN THE NEIGHBORHOOD

The Case Western Reserve tennis courts were at the top of Cedar Hill at Euclid Heights Boulevard. We would walk down to the courts and play tennis during the summer. —*Sally Slater Wilson*

TENNIS: LOTS OF LOVE IN CLEVELAND

In 1964, Roxboro School's new 7,500-seat tennis stadium in Cleveland Heights was the site of the Davis Cup final. Australia defeated the United States, 3-2, for the Cup that year. Four championship matches for the international tennis competition were held in Cleveland, in 1964, 1969, 1970 and 1973.

SPECIAL DRIVING RANGE

My fondest memory of Westlake is the night of August 4, 1972 when I met my future wife, Pat, at Silver Tee driving range and ice cream stand. She lived in North Olmsted. We started dating, and got married June 26, 1976, at St. Richard's in North Olmsted. We both have many great memories, but this one is tops. —Dave Vogt

GOLF GALORE

I remember Little Met Golf Course in the valley (Rocky River Reservation). I golfed at Little Met when I was 17 or 18. It's a nice, very pretty course, but we didn't play there that much. We also used to golf at McKinley School in Lakewood, on the gravel. One time somebody hit the ball and just missed the window in the school, missed it by about an inch.

There was someplace on Center Ridge Road, a miniature golf place near a Dairy Queen, where we used to play. But we were mainly about baseball. We were always looking for a game. —Dave Davis

GOLFING GIRLS: Getting in some miniature golf practice at Parmadale in 1961, Parma.

(continued)

smells. Most of these were aromas you smelled only at the stadium, like the combination of stale beer and mustard. The smell isn't the same at newer facilities; maybe Cleveland Stadium's old cracked concrete and rusted steel had something to do with it.

Another smell I associate with the stadium is cigars. You could bet someone sitting nearby at a Tribe game would be puffing away on an old stogy. None of my friends or family smoked cigars, so because I associated cigar smoke with attending Indians games at the stadium, whenever I smell one today, I'm instantly reminded of those days at Cleveland Municipal Stadium nearly 50 years ago.

—Alan Hitchcox

INDIANS TICKETS FROM THE GROCERY STORE

At Fisher Foods in Cleveland Heights, if you collected $50 in grocery receipts, they would give you Indians tickets. I think they just did it for a year or two. I remember standing with a bunch of my friends outside of Fisher's, asking shoppers if we could have their store receipts. I think I went to six or seven games that year, all courtesy of Fisher Foods.

—Walt Wagner

GHOST OF SUMMERS PAST: *The Red Mill* was a summer 1951 performance at Cain Park in Cleveland Heights.

Our Summer Culture

Throughout the decades, Cleveland has offered a summer's worth of cultural experiences, with both indoor and outdoor activities. Venues included Musicarnival, opened in 1954 with musicals and concerts under its tent, and Blossom Music Center, which opened in 1968 with its choice of lawn or pavilion seats that allowed us to enjoy a sense of the season while we were listening to music. Children who loved to read took part in citywide summer reading programs offered by local libraries. Seasonal theater options were many, ranging across the county, from Berea Summer Theatre to Chagrin Valley Little Theatre's summer performances and more.

Musicarnival

When Musicarnival opened in 1954 with John L. Price as producer/director, the 1,500-set venue was one of the country's first tent theaters. It was located at 4401 Warrensville Center Road, Warrensville Heights. Musicals included *South Pacific* and *West Side Story*. In later years, rock groups appeared at Musicarnival as well, including Frank Zappa and the Mothers of Invention, and Led Zeppelin in the summer of 1969. Musicarnival closed in 1975.

MUSICARNIVAL MEMORY

A favorite part of my summer was my parents taking me to see the shows at Musicarnival in Warrensville. The tent was awesome and the shows were wonderful. I remember seeing old favorites like *Carousel* and *Oklahoma*. When it rained on the tent, it was a unique experience. The voices had to soar. —*Jackie Finn*

SUMMER STAGE: Venues like Musicarnival (this is a 1968 ad) and Berea Summer Theater offered a summer's worth of entertainment.

Berea Summer Theatre

Berea Summer Theatre was started in 1957 at Baldwin-Wallace College, and ran until 2002.

THE INTERNATIONAL CONNECTION AT BEREA SUMMER THEATRE

> I tried out and was cast in a tremendously bit part as Mr. Beck in a Václav Havel play. When Václav Havel became president of the Czech Republic, I was one of the few people I knew who could say they'd actually done a Václav Havel play. It was called *The Increased Difficulty of Concentration*. I was just a guy who walked on in a trench coat and hat.
>
> —Joe Gunderman

Cain Park Theater

When Cain Park amphitheater opened in Cleveland Heights in 1938, it was the country's first municipally owned outdoor theater. Cain Park has always offered a slice of local life. In fact, in 1939—several years before she joined WEWS Channel 5—renowned news commentator Dorothy Fuldheim had a role in one of the year's productions, *The Warrior's Husband*. At the time, she was a news commentator on the ABC Radio Network; it wasn't until 1947 that she joined Channel 5. A few years later, in 1941, Cleveland industrial designer and sculptor Viktor Schreckengost designed the sets for *Divorcons*. In 1942, he designed the set for *Right You Are*. Born in 1906, Schreckengost was presented with the National Medal of Arts in 2006.

A CAIN PARK MEMORY FROM THE '50S

> The summer of 1951, before I went off to study theater at Kent State, I did summer stock at Cain Park theater. David Shaber was prop manager. He was majoring in playwriting at Yale, became a screenwriter of such films as *The Warriors*, and did a movie called *Those Lips, Those Eyes* about a theater troupe at Cain Park. Robert Ellenstein did comedy leads and went on to movies and TV. He's one of the villains in *North by Northwest*.
>
> That season one of the amphitheater's four plays was *The Red Mill*, and every night for its finale, I put on white greasepaint and a flowing gown and

SOUTH PACIFIC MEETS CHAGRIN VALLEY: In the summer of 1969, this was one of Chagrin Valley Little Theatre's productions.

PRAISING CAIN: Summer theater at Cain Park in Cleveland Heights has been a tradition since the late 1930s. Above: The stage was hot, and so was the show when *The Baker's Wife* was offered during the 1986 season at Cain Park.

as the mill's ghost popped out center stage for a big kiss from Ellenstein, who was bald but rather nice-looking.

Among other bit parts, I was one of four prostitutes in *On the Town*, along with dancer Sheila Smith, who in her last year at Kent dropped out and went off to New York for a long and successful stage career. One of her first breaks was touring with Tallulah Bankhead. Afternoons, I appeared in the popular fairy tale productions directed by Dina Rees Evans. Striking the main sets lasted well into the night. When I did occasionally show up at home, my father said, "So that's what my daughter looks like."

—Bonnie Jacobson

A CAIN PARK MEMORY FROM THE '80S

Nancy Hudson Snell recalls the summer of 1986 when she played Genevieve, the baker's wife, in the musical *The Baker's Wife*, at Cain Park in Cleveland Heights.

For an actor, the intimacy of performing at Cain Park theater can't be compared with any other theater performance. It was a lovely way to spend the summer, with mostly local actors, and a wonderful connection for me. To be that close to the audience was nice. In a large house, it's harder work because you're trying to reach the back row. For me, it was also more real, because the people were right there.

The Baker's Wife at the Alma Theater was in 1986; it's been 27 years, and it's funny that I still remember the big black drapes, hung all around

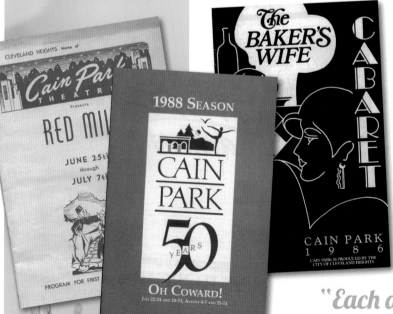

it. That's an image I have in my mind—an old brick building upstairs, the black drapes, the lighting, and it was very hot. There were no problems, but we were sweating at every performance. The thing about the Alma Theater is, in a city like Cleveland, who wants to be indoors in the summer? To be able to be outdoors for an evening of theater is awesome. Once the weather turns, we want to be outside. Each day of summer is like a little candy-box gift, a wrapped present that we get, to go outside and watch a concert, a musical, or a play.

—Nancy Hudson Snell

"Each day of summer is like a little candy-box gift."

Great Lakes Shakespeare Festival

The Great Lakes Shakespeare Festival, later known as the Great Lakes Theater Festival, launched its first season on July 11, 1962, offering six Shakespeare plays at Lakewood Civic Auditorium. By 1965, the Festival broadened its selection of plays to other classics as well as Shakespearean plays. Students at Lakewood High School attended performances with their English classes to see *Macbeth* and *A Midsummer Night's Dream* in the fall of 1965. Directors in the early years included Arthur Lithgow (1962-1965), Lawrence Carra (1966-1975), Vincent Dowling (1976-1984) and Gerald Freedman (1985). In 1982, the Great Lakes Theater Festival moved to the Ohio Theatre downtown.

THE BARD AND DRINKS IN THE YARD: An opening night reception at the Great Lakes Shakespeare Festival, June 30, 1964, outside Lakewood Civic Auditorium.

A GREAT LAKES SHAKESPEARE FESTIVAL MEMORY

When the Great Lakes Shakespeare Festival was at Lakewood Civic Auditorium, my sister Colette was an usher. She actually ended up being one of the backstage theater assistants, too. In their production of Shakespeare's *A Midsummer Night's Dream* (1973), she was Cobweb. We had the cobweb prop hanging out in our basement for a long time. Larry Carra was there at the time.

—*Joe Gunderman*

Music Under the Stars and Elsewhere

While The Beatles concert at Cleveland Municipal Stadium on August 14, 1966 made a big splash, most baby boomers remember the World Series of Rock that began eight years later. With its seating capacity of more than 78,000 and ticket prices that started at $8, this series at Cleveland Municipal Stadium kicked off on July 23, 1974. At that event, 33,000 fans showed up to hear The Beach Boys, Joe Walsh, REO Speedwagon, and Lynyrd Skynyrd. Meanwhile, at Cain Park Amphitheater during the 1970s, WJW radio was broadcasting live from the park, and on Rock-n-Roll Fridays, up to 5,000 teens showed up to hear live bands.

Come In, It's Cool Inside

In the 1930s and 1940s, movie theaters were a great place to beat the summer heat because they were the only public places that were air conditioned.

—*Joe Valencic*

SUMMER MOVIES

In the summer, I remember riding our bikes to the Shaker movie theater, which had children's matinees every Saturday. There were always yo-yo contests in addition to cartoons and short subjects and features. There was always some sort of a prize giveaway. So it was always fun to walk to the Shaker theater to enjoy this on a weekly basis. On the way we'd always stop at Vinnie's Hardware and Toy Store and look at the latest toys that came in.

—*Dennis Gaughan*

LAST PICTURE SHOW

I have the very last ticket ever purchased at the Vogue Theater in Shaker Heights. I was there on its last day with my friend, and wanted to be the last customer. I was a kid, and it was summer.

—*Fred Taub*

BEATLES AT MUNICIPAL STADIUM

My sister is seven years older than me and would sometimes allow me to tag along with her to concerts. That is how I got to see the Beatles at Municipal Stadium in August of 1966 when I was nine years old. I remember all the people rushing down into the field from the stands, but I wouldn't leave the seats. My sister was stuck with me up there but was somewhat consoled when some guys told her they could get her Beatles cigarette butts. She still has some of them (wink, wink) in the little bag they brought to her. Our parents picked us up outside afterwards and we still can't figure out how they found us in the crowd. —*Suzanne DeGaetano*

BEATLES AS SUMMER MEMORY

My favorite Cleveland memory takes me back to August 14, 1966, and my very first visit to Cleveland Stadium. But it wasn't baseball that brought me to the stadium that night. Far from it. After enduring much crying, begging, and pleading, my parents finally gave consent for their 13-year-old daughter to go see the Beatles in concert! I couldn't believe it. I wasn't going to listen to them on my transistor radio, play their album on my record player or watch them on Ed Sullivan. No, this time was much different. This time my favorite group was coming to Cleveland and I was going to see them sing in person! I used my babysitting money and purchased my $5.50 ticket.

READY TO ROLL: And ready to rock, at this July 1972 music festival.

My parents gave me strict instructions about the concert. They would drop my cousin Connie and me off and pick us up afterward. I was not to leave my seat for any reason, and I was to meet them promptly after the concert.

I bought my souvenir program, and we made our way to our seats. The concert was incredible. I could barely hear the Beatles among all the screaming and crying going on around me. I couldn't tell you what songs they sang. I couldn't tell you what they were wearing or what they said between songs. I couldn't tell you who the warm-up acts were. I couldn't tell you if I was also screaming and crying. It didn't matter that it was a lousy sound system. I was there. I was seeing John, Paul, George, and Ringo in concert! Right in my town! I was mesmerized by it all.

Girls by the hundreds started rushing up to the stage. I certainly was tempted to get a closer look at Paul myself, but I remembered what I had promised my parents, and I also didn't want to get trampled. Connie, on the other hand, made no such promise and told me she had to go find Paul, and off she went. I was sitting by myself and wondering what to do if she couldn't find her way back to where I was sitting. Eventually, she came back, and she was crying and claiming Paul had looked right at her.

We had the best time. I don't know how we ever met up with my parents, I was so giddy with excitement of seeing the Beatles. The Boys from Liverpool had come to my home town. And I was there! It is by far my most cherished Cleveland summer memory. —*Joanie Hitchcox*

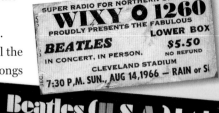

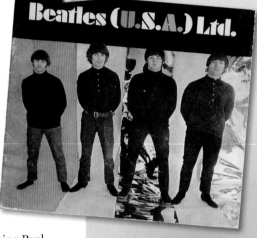

FAB FOUR SOUVENIRS: Ticket and program from the Beatles concert at Municipal Stadium in the summer of 1966.

WHEN PIGS FLEW

The old Cleveland Stadium hosted many concerts in the 1970s. I had made a hobby of seeing live concerts with my friends, and we weren't about to miss Pink Floyd playing at the stadium. It was packed to capacity, and we had nosebleed seats. From our vantage point, the giant, grunting red-eyed pig that floated across the top of the stadium on an invisible line seemed to be coming to get us. The concert began with the roar of a jet engine that flew low, directly overhead. Perhaps it was enhanced by the sound system, because it was deafening. The light show and fireworks were spectacular. That is, by far, the best concert I ever attended. —*Laurie Ghetia-Orr*

"She was crying and claiming Paul had looked right at her."

MUSIC NOTES: DID YOU ATTEND ANY OF THESE SUMMER CONCERTS?

- August 14, 1966, at Cleveland Municipal Stadium: The Beatles

- July 14, 1968, at Musicarnival: The Who, in a concert featuring one of Pete Townshend's documented guitar-smashes (a Fender Stratocaster)

- July 23, 1968, at Blossom Music Center: Judy Collins and Arlo Guthrie are the first pop artists to perform at this venue during its opening season, part of the summer's Jazz-Folk series

- August 29, 1969, at Blossom Music Center: Janis Joplin and the Faces

- June 23, 1974, at Cleveland Municipal Stadium: first World Series of Rock concert (The Beach Boys, Lynyrd Skynyrd, REO Speedwagon, and Joe Walsh)

- July 10, 1975, at Richfield Coliseum: Elvis Presley drew 22,000 fans the year after this venue opened

- July 1, 1978, at Cleveland Municipal Stadium: The Rolling Stones attracted 82,500 for this World Series of Rock event

- August 25, 1982, at Blossom Music Center: Michael Stanley Band drew more than 74,000 attendees during the four nights they played that August (25, 26, 30 and 31).

- June 20, 1987, at Nautica Stage: Southside Johnny and the Asbury Jukes were Belkin Productions' opening concert at Cleveland's permanent outdoor theater on the Cuyahoga River

LOOK UP!

The stadium concert I went to see was Pink Floyd. Everybody who went to that concert will tell you the same story. They're waiting for the band to go on, waiting for the band to go on, and all of a sudden a jet plane flies over the stadium. Everybody looks up. And as soon as the jet plane flew over, which took three seconds, boom, the first note was hit. No one saw them go onstage because everybody looked up. It was brilliant. —*Steve Presser*

WORKING AT THE WORLD SERIES OF ROCK, JULY 1980

I belonged to the stagehands union. One summer I got a union call to help build the stage for the World Series of Rock at Cleveland Municipal Stadium. The bands were Bob Seger & the Silver Bullet Band, The J. Geils Band, Eddie Money and Def Leppard.

We workers were stripped to the waist, wearing shorts and hammers in holsters, under a blazing sun. We clung like spiders to the web of steel as we erected scaffolding, first for the large stage, raised about 10 feet above center field, and then multi-story towers of scaffolding to support the immense stage roof truss. Every so often, the fork lift driver who was hoisting sections up to us would bump the scaffold base and we held on as the steel towers swayed. It was hard and dangerous work before we had a lot of the OSHA safety rules there are now.

The day of the concert, large cubes of dry ice had to be hauled up the scaffolding to cool the massive stacks of Crown power amps for the speaker stacks. Shirtless stage hands got burned carrying the dry ice up on their shoulders.

Just before the show, the stage manager told me to grab a box of colored Frisbees and go out and start hurling them into the crowd to get people cranked up for the show. I walked out on stage and caught the attention of 80,000-plus people and started throwing Frisbees. The crowd roared and went crazy trying to catch them. When that wall of sound hit me, I realized why performing live is so addictive. Talk about adrenaline! —*Stephen Bellamy*

Blossom Music Center Blooms in 1968

When the Cleveland Orchestra performed its first piece (*The Star-Spangled Banner*) at Blossom Music Center's inaugural concert—conducted by George Szell on July 19, 1968—it started a tradition for Northeast Ohioans who embrace open-air music. Blossom Music Center was built by the Cleveland Orchestra's parent organization, the Musical Arts Association, and named for longtime

LAWN SEATS: Concert-goers on the lawn at Blossom Music Center.

GROUND-BREAKING: Frank Joseph, Mrs. Dudley S. Blossom Sr. and Betsy Blossom (granddaughter) at the Blossom Music Center ground-breaking ceremony on July 2, 1967.

orchestra-supporters the Blossom family. The 800-acre site, surrounded by Cuyahoga Valley National Park in Cuyahoga Falls, seats 5,700 concertgoers in its pavilion, and 13,500 on the lawn. Groundbreaking ceremonies took place on July 2, 1967.

During its opening year, Blossom Music Center also featured a Jazz-Folk 1968 concert series with Judy Collins, Arlo Guthrie, Herb Alpert and the Tijuana Brass, Ravi Shankar, and other big names of the era.

PHOTO OP AT BLOSSOM

My sister took me to my first concert at Blossom. It was to see Glen Campbell and it must have been sometime in the early 1970s. I went to Blossom many times after that, most recently with friends to see the Orchestra. My mom loved concerts, and I remember sitting in the Pavilion with her to see Tony Bennett and, years later, Mary Chapin Carpenter.

One evening sticks out in my mind, but I can't remember the act. I was with a bunch of high school girlfriends and as we were walking from our car to the show we spotted the perfect photo op: seven or eight motorcycles parked together. We arranged ourselves on the bikes and somewhere there is a picture of this—a beautiful summer evening in the parking lot of Blossom in the mid-1970s, smiling teenage girls atop bikes that were not theirs. —*Suzanne DeGaetano*

MUSIC ON THE SLOPES

I can remember many a beautiful night attending concerts on the grassy slopes of Blossom Music Center, relaxing to the sounds of great music.
—*Sally Slater Wilson*

SOUNDS OF THE '60S: Cleveland's blossoming outdoor music scene came into its own when Blossom Music Center opened in 1968, with the Cleveland Orchestra summer concerts and a Jazz-Folk Concert Series. The Janis Joplin Show rocked in 1969.

POETS, PLAY BALL!

It's true that poets have an affinity for baseball. This usually consists of writing about it, talking about it, and watching it. But in the summer of 1982 a handful of poets took the bold step of actually playing it. The Poets' League of Greater Cleveland (known later as the Poets' & Writers' League, and finally, as The Lit), of which I was a member, played three softball games that summer. I pitched five innings for the Poets against the West Side Therapists at Forest Hill Park in Cleveland Heights.

I thought our lineup was pretty impressive. We had Bob McDonough and John Donoghue, Brooklyn natives who had actually gone to Dodgers games at Ebbets Field. Cy Dostal was a chain smoker and not exactly light on his feet, but he had a good arm. Carolyn Donoghue could hit, throw, and catch. I ran five days a week, so in case I connected with the ball, I could get to base quickly. The therapists appeared to be in very good shape, but I thought they lacked focus.

The first batter got a hit and went to first. The second, a wild swinger, struck out. The third batter hit a short fly. I put up my glove and—smack! I caught it and threw to second. Three outs and the poets were up. We scored, and the therapists got competitive. I heard one of them mutter, "Are we going to let ourselves get beaten by a bunch of poets?"

—*Meredith Holmes*

Calling All Literature-Lovers

Once school was out, summer offered the perfect opportunity for recreational reading. Some kids took advantage of summer reading programs offered by local libraries.

SUMMER READING GAMES IN SOUTH EUCLID AND MAYFIELD

When I was going into second grade, I played the summer reading game at our South Euclid branch. I loved to read, and spent all summer reading. Of course, I was reading small, first readers at the time. I would sit on a swing in my backyard and read all day. I read over 90 first readers that summer. At the summation of the game in August, my name was announced along with the number of books I had read. The woman standing next to my mother scoffed, "That girl didn't read that many books!" Needless to say, my mother had a few choice words for her.

As I got older, we went to the Mayfield Library, where my brother, my best friend, her brother, and I would attend creative writing and book discussions throughout the summer. I still have my creative writing booklets from that time. Back then, the summer reading game was like a board game, where you landed on a spot and had to read what was suggested. I know that literature now says that open reading is best, but I loved landing on spaces and reading books I otherwise would not have. —*Maria Trivisonno*

READING IN WEST PARK AND BEREA

My mom was a voracious mystery reader and we visited the library once a week (when my dad was available, as we only had one car). The West Park branch of Cleveland Public Library was a lovely old-fashioned looking building with a rotunda in the middle where the checkout desk was, the adult wing on one side and the children's room on the other. The ceilings were very high and you really needed to be quiet or your voice would resonate. I had a special relationship with the children's librarian—I think I had a goal of reading all of the books in her room.

During the summer reading game we "reported" about the books we read and the librarian made a list of them on our game card. It looks like we had a goal of reading 10 books. I believe the Rockport branch was opened during this time and was closer to our home, but we continued to visit the West Park branch. This was during the time I was age six to nine.

READING INTO IT: What was on the page was all the rage at summer reading clubs sponsored by local libraries.

In the summer of 1964 we moved to Middleburg Heights and I saved a card from the summer of 1965 from the Berea Branch of the Cuyahoga County Public Library. My dad had to drive us from Middleburg Heights to Berea to go to the library, since the Middleburg Heights branch was not built until 1969. —*Carol Evans Abel*

CLEVELAND PUBLIC LIBRARY

I used to love to go downtown to the Cleveland Public Library, which was my idea of a good time. —*Sam Bell*

Cleveland offered many other cultural experiences, too. Cleveland Public Schools sponsored a garden program in the summer, and the Cleveland Museum of Art's summer art classes made the summer more memorable.

GROWING IN THE GARDEN

My mom remembered the garden project, and talked about it for 50 years after we participated, so it must have been a big thing. Since it was part of the science curriculum, my classroom teacher stopped at the house and "graded" my garden. I remember being introduced to marigolds through this program, as I have vivid memories of planting those dart-like seeds and the pungent smell of the marigolds when I pinched off spent flowers.
—*Carol Abel*

THE ART OF WADE PARK LAGOON

In the 1950s, I took art classes in the summer at the Cleveland Museum of Art. They were usually six-week classes, meeting once a week, and you would do work in University Circle, specifically Wade Park Lagoon. You would take your water colors, paints or drawings and go out and do your sketches. It was a wonderful thing to take advantage of a cultural institution, and be exposed to the great Cleveland Museum of Art every summer. The Wade Park Lagoon area was so well-maintained—the flower beds and the pond area were pristine. You'd go under a shady tree, set up your easel and do whatever you wanted to do.

The museum's art instructors were very encouraging, and we were with groups of kids of all different skill levels. There was never a sense of competition. That was another great thing the museum fostered: encouraging a person to experiment.
—*Dennis Gaughan*

Willing Summer Learners

SUMMER SCHOOL AT WEST TECH

Most students who attended summer school did so because they had failed a course during the regular school year. I attended summer school at West Tech High School for two years because I wanted to take extra courses that I could not fit into my regular school-year schedule. I took American History and Government during the summer of 1958, after completing my sophomore year at West Tech. The next summer, after completing my junior year, I took English Literature and Trigonometry. Because I also took the maximum number of courses during the regular school year, I accumulated enough points to graduate early, but I chose to stay in school and graduate with my class of June 1960. Attending summer school meant getting up very early in the morning, but still having the remainder of the day for summertime fun.

—*Lois Gollwitzer Dixon*

SUMMER SCHOOL IN LAKEWOOD

My memories of summer include summer school at Lincoln Elementary School. It was more like day camp, and a lot more fun than school.

—*Helen Wirt*

CLEVELAND PUBLIC SCHOOLS

SCHOOL GARDEN EXHIBIT

MERIT AWARD

CELLENT

CLEVELAND PUBLIC SCHOOLS
GARDEN EXHIBIT

Name CAROL EVANS
Room or Group No. 113   Class No. 32
Article Exhibited MARIGOLD
Excellent Very Good Good Honorable Mention

SPOKES KIDS: A 1967 Memorial Day street parade in Cleveland Heights kicked off with decorated bicycles.

KID STUFF

Fun in the Neighborhood

For many of us, Cleveland summers ran the gamut of activity-filled days of swimming, summer school, softball, bike-riding and exploring the neighborhood. For others, it meant lazy afternoons reading library books on the front porch swing while waiting for the paperboy to swing by—crouching with one knee in his newspaper-filled Radio Flyer wagon as he used his other foot to push his way along the street. There was nothing quite like reading the funnies with Dick Tracy and Archie in the comics section of the *Cleveland News* afternoon paper while eating messy penny candy such as Lik-M-Aid, "the candy that pours." If you were an entrepreneurial type, you probably had a summer job, maybe even a year-round paper route. Other enterprising kids operated lemonade stands, returned pop bottles to get the two-cent deposit for spending money, or sold tickets to the backyard carnivals they staged.

Once a summer, block parties rolled around, often prompting hastily assembled parades and bike rallies with decorated Schwinns, Murrays, and Raleigh English racers.

Mostly, though, summer in Cleveland was a time when summer days flowed into summer nights, with a spirit of adventure and enthusiasm for the riches that were right there in front of us.

C'MON IN, THE WATER'S FINE:
Backyard pools ruled.

Summer 1961

SUMMER DAYS

No one stayed inside. Outside called to us all in those mid-1950s South Euclid summers, from first light until after street lamps came on and held us in their warm spell even when it rained. Summer mornings, Princeton Boulevard neighborhood kids spilled from front stoops, with younger brothers and sisters following older ones out onto fescued lawns, backyard swing sets and hot paved driveways. Chalked hopscotches decorated sidewalks while "Mother-May-I" lines appeared on concrete aprons with squealing players dashing madly back trying not to be tagged by the kid who was "Mother."

Girls playing "dress-up" paraded in front yards, tripping on long house-dresses that bloused over flat chests—straw or wool mushroom hats topping the whole look. We discovered roller skating was the best when we reached the downhill run of smooth slate sidewalks on Greenvale Road that intersected Princeton. We'd glide past the Little Leaguers practicing on the ballfield on the far side of Lowden School, hoping not to trip on the uneven slabs, but of course that always happened and for three months, our skinned legs and elbows carried the surest sign that summer was here: red-orange merthiolate stains. Mothers dripped it on our wounds with brown glass droppers, then blew on the scrapes to make the sting stop.

—*Bunny Breslin*

SUMMER NIGHTS

Summer nights when I was a child in the 1950s involved fireflies and playing with the boys in the empty lot where second base was a tree. My older brother taught me how to not "throw like a girl" before I knew that doing anything like a girl was quite okay. Toward the end of the summer we switched to football and I got to wear his red leather shoulder pads, never really learning the rules of football except how to hold the ball with the stitches against my palm and spin it as I threw.

Summer nights when I was a teenager in the 1960s, my girlfriends and I bicycled on the smooth asphalt streets from house to house of friends, helmetless and hands off the handlebars, landing on cool green lawns to visit with the boys. When the boys started to drive, they would stop at my house because my mother cleverly always had ice cream for our milkshake machine. The boys would come for milkshakes and the girls for the boys. I learned the sound of a particular blue Rambler, could hear it coming down the street and held my breath waiting for it to stop in my driveway with the one who came for me, not the milkshakes. I remember him walking up to the front door, shoes in one hand and an apple in another. When he left without his shoes, I knew he'd be back.

One summer night the police stopped us because he was driving too slow, his arm around my shoulders and head leaning into mine. —*Peggy Spaeth*

FREE-RANGE KIDS

The best part of summer was freedom. We might have been one of the last generations of free-range kids. When I was six or seven, I would find old pop bottles and walk down to Mike's Deli, across the street from Kensington grade school on Lake Road in Rocky River. I would trade them in for candy. I would mostly walk down with a sibling or friend, but I can remember going by myself, which is unheard-of anymore. —*Noreen Hone*

SUMMER ON YOUR OWN STREET

Summer on Rockway Avenue in Lakewood during the 1960s is one of those memories that just keeps coming back. What always strikes me about returning to my childhood home is the proximity of the houses to each other. During a game of hide-and-seek when school was just out, that layout provided countless hiding spots for the more than 100 kids who often joined in the game.

Later, you could always count on one or more classmates to host a practically round-the-clock front porch game of Monopoly. There were at least three stellar tree houses within four houses of mine and with the right attitude on display, you could always get someone to throw down the rope ladder.

SUMMER SPENDING MONEY: If you had a paper route for the *Cleveland Press*, the *Cleveland Plain Dealer* or the *Cleveland News*, you learned how to make change and earned extra spending money for summer fun.

SUPER: Superman grew more sophisticated as we did, from the early comics created by Clevelanders Joe Shuster and Jerry Siegel in the 1930s to pastimes like the Superman Video Arcade game by Taito, popular in 1988.

GOOD YARD WORK NEVER HURT ANYBODY: Unless cutting the grass interfered with your other plans for the day.

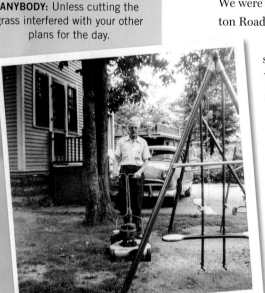

Before anybody knew what a Metropark was, some kid would ride up on a Sting-Ray and yell, "Hey! Let's go to the valley." We'd form up on the leader, ride down Riverside Drive, drop down into the park at Sharky's Hill, and find a shallow spot to cross the river. Expeditions would sometimes end at Eddie's Boat Dock refreshment stand, or maybe stretch out in the other direction to Bagley Road and civilization. Without the benefit of a paved jogging/bike path, we blazed our own trail in the style of Lewis and Clark. My street was the envy of St. James parish, and I still hear from kids who recall crashing our block party to hear The Paupers rock on my parents' front porch. —*George Ghetia*

MOSQUITO-CHASERS

We could walk to a little store on West Avenue at West 134th (it has been made into a home) where we bought "mosquito chasers"—thin sticks about 10 inches long. There was something on the stick that, when lit, burned very slowly and repelled mosquitoes. It was almost like a cattail in miniature, about 10 inches long and only 1/4-inch thick. —*Carol Evans Abel*

GAMES IN CLEVELAND HEIGHTS

Our favorite hiding spot was atop the far side of Dr. O'Malley's garage roof. We were the hunted in teams of "cops and robbers" who took over Demington Road after early summer dinners, until dusk.

The Callaghan, Hanrahan, Mullally, Krieger, and Coakley kids spread out over a quarter-mile stretch of finely manicured lawns. We were marauders hiding and seeking in trees, hedges, tool sheds, and flower gardens.

The adult residents were comfortable with our trespassing games. They knew each of us by name, might have been paying closer attention than we realized, and understood that when the mosquitos started biting, the noisy games would end.

They called Demington Road "pill hill," for all the doctors who lived there. I don't remember anyone ever needing their services.

—*Christy Callaghan McLaughlin*

"The adult residents were comfortable with our trespassing games."

SUBURBAN SAFARIS

In the 1950s, during the summer months, my friends and I would explore the Roxboro ravine running between North Park and Fairhill, looking for the scary hermit we were told lived in a cave down there. These suburban safaris were always punctuated with shouts of, "There he is!" followed by lots of screaming and scrambling up hills. Of course, we never saw the apocryphal gentleman in question.

—*Christine Howey*

SCHOOL SWINGS INTO SUMMER: Girls on the playground at Hathaway Brown School, 1980.

THE SECOND-DUMBEST THING I DID DURING MY SUMMER VACATION

It is a truism that the American suburbs of the early 1960s were a sterile, stifling, and unexciting environment for the zillions of baby-boomer kids living in them. But you can't prove that by me or the other Bellamy boys and girls. Adventurous risk was wherever you could find it—and we often found it in disquieting places. Consider this typical summer scene from my early adolescence. It's cold. It's damp. It's dark. It's really scary. And it smells like a sewer, as it should, for my brothers Christopher and Stephen and I, and our sister Nicole are walking inside a clammy storm sewer several hundred feet northeast of Cedar Hill Baptist Church in Cleveland Heights, maybe 15 feet underground. We think, or perhaps merely hope, that this sewer leads to an outlet in Dugway Creek at Lake View Cemetery. We know we're not supposed to be there, but we can't stop ourselves. It's dangerous, it's thrilling, and it's forbidden. How could any child of the suburbs resist?

Not that we don't believe we know what we're about. As always, brother Stephen, 14, leads the way, the Captain Kirk of our exploratory squad. Thanks to his presumed expertise, the result of years of rubbernecking municipal maintenance workers and construction gangs, we're equipped for any contingency imaginable to our youthful minds. Sporting rubber boots and raincoats, we carry heavy-duty flashlights and coils of seriously thick rope. I'm 13, Christopher is 12, and Nicole is all of nine, and we are once again Stephen's foot soldiers on another forbidden escapade. Well, maybe not technically, but it would be forbidden if our parents had any inkling of our perilous doings.

Although we won't admit it, we are all terrified, and not just because we know we're doing something forbidden. And we're not really scared by the thought of being caught by concerned citizens or the cops. No, the specter

HAVING A BLAST: Edgewater Park in 1978.

that haunts us as we trudge downward is the fear of what might—nay, must happen if it should start raining while we're . . . down here. Other kids, we know, even children from the secure precincts of Cleveland Heights, have drowned while pursuing explorations such as this. But we can't admit to ourselves, much less each other, just how frightened we are as the beams of our flashlights stab into the mephitic gloom.

It's probably no more than 10 minutes after we enter the culvert that we hear the first ominous rumble. "Was that . . . was that . . . thunder?"

We stop, paralyzed and speechless. Two heartbeats pass, and I start to say, "No, you're just being para-," when a second clap reverberates down the tunnel's walls. Stephen spins around, and I realize as I stare into his eerily flashlit face that's he's thinking what I'm thinking: If something happens to our little nine-year-old sister Nicole, facing our parents will be a far worse fate than mere drowning.

He doesn't even have to issue the command to turn around. Just as the first trickle from the thunderstorm begins dribbling down the pipe under our feet, we wheel about as one, and begin scrambling and scuttling back up toward the open ravine and safety. The storm water is already churning a foot-wide path as we splash, panic-stricken and panting, to the opening just south of Derbyshire Road. Suddenly, we're outside in the pouring rain, gasping and gulping air, deliriously happy to be alive.

I wish I could tell you that we learned our lesson that '60s summer night. But that would be a lie. We never returned to the sewers and we never took Nicole on any more harebrained expeditions. But we learned nothing else from the experience.

A year later, inspired by the subterranean exploits dramatized by Steve McQueen et al. in *The Great Escape*, we . . . well, you can read about that disaster in *The Last Days of Cleveland*.

Informed, some decades later, of our childhood misadventures, my mother would only say—like many a parent, past, present, and future—"I'm glad I didn't know." —*John Stark Bellamy II*

A highly altered account of this misadventure appeared in the May 2002 edition of *Northern Ohio Live*.

SPLASHY, SWINGING GOOD TIMES: Summer meant getting back to nature in your own yard.

Life from the Front Porch

Activities didn't need to be far-flung to be fun. Sometimes just hanging out in your own yard was entertainment enough for a summer's day in Cleveland.

POOR BARBIE

We spent hours playing a game we invented, "Barbie High Dives." We filled buckets with water and threw Barbie dolls off the porch into the buckets in the front yard. The winner was the one who got Barbie into the bucket the most times. When we would get tired of this game, we removed Barbie's head and laughed like crazy, saying, "I have a splitting headache." Then we'd throw the buckets of water at each other to cool off on a hot summer day.
—*Laura Wirt-Budny*

MOVIE STARS ON THE FRONT PORCH

We didn't do as many organized activities as kids today. We played at home in the yard and on the front porch. We made-up games like "Movie Stars." One person thought of the name of a movie star or a TV program. They stood on the sidewalk and the rest of us sat on the front porch steps and tried to guess who the star was, or what program they were thinking of.

DIG IT: Sandboxes brought a bit of the beach to the backyard.

The person who guessed correctly jumped off the porch and chased the other person across the yard to the hedge by the driveway. If they tagged the person, then they got to be the one who thought up the movie star or TV program. If they didn't catch the person, I guess that first person got to be "it" again. I think this was a Baukema family original game.

Some other fun games we used to play were "Mother, May I?" and "Telephone." We also played with hula hoops and went roller skating on the neighborhood sidewalks.

We enjoyed playing on the front porch. We played board games and dress-up. We used old clothes and curtains for dress up.

We played a lot of pretend games in the basement. I remember playing house, school, church, and funeral home. We had an opening in the wall between the furnace room and the main part of the basement. My sister and I would put on puppet shows. —*Laura Riccardi*

Backyard Blasts

Backyards were for swimming pools, kid carnivals, and catching lightning bugs. Oh, and sometimes for mischief, too.

BACKYARD SWIMMING POOL

My dad's store—Hollywood Cleaners—was in Rocky River, just a bicycle ride down Wooster Road, right next to the Westlake Hotel, not far from where we lived. Then we moved to a house around the corner on South Sagamore, where my dad put in a kidney-shaped in-ground swimming pool. The pool was one of the nice things in the neighborhood, and we had a lot of people over. My dad wanted the pool for swimming—he had had some back problems—and we did laps in the pool, all through the summer and into October or November. —*Howard Schwartz*

BUILDING A BACKYARD CARNIVAL

We made backyard carnivals with wild wagon rides, fun houses made out of cardboard boxes, and an obstacle course that included garbage cans, barbecue grills, and hula hoops. —*Laura Wirt-Budny*

SURREY DOWN SUMMER

The Breslins were an inventive lot and, as the kids grew older, my brother, sister, and I designed summer carnivals for everyone who could pay a nickel to come to visit. We made posters that we thumbtacked to lamp posts around the neighborhood and told everyone when the carnival would be.

On the carnival day, other kids helped take nickels at the back gate or judged one of the contests and, even with all those helpers, there were still many kids who came.

All around the edge of the backyard there were games and activities: "go-fish" in a small plastic pool, tossing tennis balls through an inner tube, musical chairs, hula-hoop contests, flipping cards. One summer there was a marionette show in the Breslin basement.

We also had a "carnival special" we called the Amazing Frog Girl. My sister Betty remembers being covered with a sheet, sitting underneath with her leg wrapped around her neck. Then when a patron would come by, my brother Bill or I would rip off the sheet and Frog-Girl Betty would get up and hop around until the sheet went back on.

DOUBLE DIPPING: Whether it was two kids or more, backyard pools were perfect for taking a dip on a hot afternoon.

But the best carnival was the surrey summer of 1960. Christmas of 1959 had brought a grand surprise for the Breslin kids. Near the tree stood a bright red-framed surrey with yellow wood seats and a red and white striped canopy edged with white fringe. It was the Gym-Dandy Surrey-With-The-Fringe-On-Top endorsed by Art Linkletter on his *House Party* show. For the summer carnival that year, we gave rides around the block to everyone who was patient enough to wait. The person in the back seat provided the pedal-power while those in the front rode along. Though it was hard to pedal, especially with two people in the front seat, it was the delight of the neighborhood. —*Bunny Breslin*

BACKYARD AMUSEMENT PARKS

We lived in Cleveland and had a small backyard. The kids in the neighborhood always tried to recreate Geauga Lake or Euclid Beach in the backyard with wagons and rides. We had refreshment stands where we would have grape juice and we tried to simulate the whole amusement park thing with attractions. We had games of chance—throwing baseballs through a hoop, and things like that. The neighborhood kids would play all day. In the summer, you'd just be out all day and there was no worry about where kids were because somebody was in somebody else's yard or riding bikes or playing "amusement park." —*Dennis Gaughan*

INNER CIRCLE: Family pools got bigger as we grew older.

Reinventing Baseball

You didn't have to play in a softball league or belong to any organizations to play summer baseball in the Cleveland area. Creative kids invented their own versions of the game.

HOME PLATE IS THE DRIVEWAY DRAIN

If I wasn't at day camp, I was at my best friend's house playing baseball in his backyard. That's what I did probably until high school. There were three or four of us at Barry Clifford's house. They had a driveway drain in the backyard that was a perfect home plate. —*Dave Davis*

"We had games of chance–throwing baseballs through a hoop, and things like that."

FRONT STEPS BASEBALL

You only needed two players to play front steps baseball. We would use a tennis ball and each player would pick a team name. One player, the batter, would throw the ball at the porch steps and the second player, the fielder, would have to field the ball as it bounced off the steps.

A catch on the fly was an out. A clean catch after the ball hit the ground was a force out. If the ball got past the fielder, it was a base hit, depending on how far the ball rolled before it was fielded.

We kept track of "men" on base, outs, and runs scored. After three outs, the teams switched positions and after nine innings, the team that scored the most runs won. —*Karl Riccardi*

PHANTOM PHUN

My son and a neighbor boy were playing ball in the backyard and his mother was in the kitchen. The kids were arguing, so we went to the door to stop it. We saw the two kids out playing ball—with no ball, no bat, no glove—and they were arguing about who hit a home run. It was all imaginary.
—*Joann Rae Macias*

Fun on Wheels

Bicycles, wagons, roller skates, and skateboards improved the mobility of adventurous children who wanted to explore the neighborhood on their own.

IN LAKEWOOD'S CLIFTON PARK NEIGHBORHOOD

As I remember it, all the kids of Clifton Park (and friends) of bike-riding age, from three or four to 15 and 16, would get together and ride over, en masse, to this house on West Clifton, as it had a four- or five-car garage with a three-car mechanical floor turn-around in it. We'd all get in the garage with our bikes—everything from little three-wheelers and Western Flyers with banana seats to Schwinn 10-speeds and of course a Red Wagon or two, or three.

Anyway, we'd all get on the turntable transportation, and someone would push the button and the whole floor would slowly turn 180 degrees. Then we'd all get back on the bikes and dash out of the garage to the street, just to turn around and drive back into the garage and do it again and again.

We did this for hours during weekdays after school for what seemed like weeks, until one day, the turntable finally broke. That was the end of our

THE KEY TO A COOL GETAWAY: On slate, concrete, or at a rink, roller skating was part of summer fun.

free rides. The folks found out what had happened to their turntable and, from then on, they locked their garage when they went to work after they put their kids' bikes out on the driveway. Good, simple, innocent, fun times.

—*Command Sergeant Major István A. Burgyán, US Army Infantry Retired*

CREATING SPARKS

We spent a lot of time riding our Schwinn banana-seat bikes and roller skating. The roller skates needed a key to tighten them. Our street was brick, and we discovered that if you held onto a rope with a friend pulling you on their bike, the roller skate wheels would create sparks from the bricks. Long before the summer was over our skate wheels would be split in half from the brick street. More of that fun would have to wait until the next summer. We usually got new roller skates in our Easter baskets the following year.

—*Laura Wirt-Budny*

THE BIKE CULTURE

I never went out on my bike in the summer without my baseball mitt hanging on the handlebars. In those days, in the middle of summer, you never saw a ballfield with nobody on it; there were pick-up games. Even if you just had four guys, you'd play two on a side and call your field. You'd play anywhere. If you had your mitt with you and you saw a bunch of kids you didn't know who didn't have many players, you could watch and sooner or later they'd see your mitt on your bicycle handlebars and ask, "You want to play?" —*Joe Gunderman*

SKATING ON SLATE

I mostly roller skated around the block, the stretch between Derbyshire and Euclid Heights Boulevard in Cleveland Heights. Berkshire Lane was almost entirely slate and it was wonderful. Other places had some rough patches that shook your brain and tingled your feet, and you couldn't wait to get over them. Then I'd come down Edgehill and would be cruising fast, dreading that I would encounter an unsuspecting pedestrian on the curve. Even smooth concrete was annoying because it was bumpy.

We also skated at St. Ann's in the basement rink, and the nuns kept a lid on things. They were adept at standing on the outer walkway and catching the arm or ear of rowdy boys. —*Nicole Loughman*

LET THE GOOD TIMES ROLL: The Schwinn Pea Picker Sting-Ray was a '70s classic.

SCHWINN STING-RAY

I had my five-speed Fastback Schwinn Sting-ray. It was really, really cool. Most often we didn't have chain locks, but one kid got his bike ripped off and that started the chain locks. Back then, you wrapped the chain locks around, and kids started getting these horrible paint nicks on their bikes. Finally, some genius came up with a chain lock that had a plastic sleeve.

—*Steve Presser*

TRUST AND A LITTLE BIT OF PIXIE DUST: A backyard performance of *Peter Pan* in Cleveland Heights, 1955, two years after the classic Disney film was released.

SHOWING THE FLAG: A street parade in Lakewood, July 4, 1954.

ROLLER RINK FUN

Every Saturday, our family of six kids would walk one mile to St. Ann's School and roller skate in the afternoon. There were scheduled races by age, and the winner would receive snacks from the snack bar. Fierce competition ensued, as many of the children did not get snacks at home.

—*Sally Slater Wilson*

Neighborhoods on July Fourth

WALKING TO SEE FIREWORKS

I lived in one of the neighborhoods close to Edgewater Park. The beach was a 15-minute walk from my house. What made the walk to the beach unique was the West 76th Street tunnel. It started at the end of West 76th Street, at the old Union Carbide plant, ran under the Shoreway, and ended at the beach at Edgewater Park. The tunnel was dank, musty, and poorly lit. It leaked rainwater. It was covered in graffiti and it smelled of urine, but it was the best way to get to the show.

On the Fourth of July, thousands of people walked through that tunnel to get to the beach, but that meant walking down West 76th Street first. West 76th Street is short and narrow and working-class. The houses are small and packed together as tightly as cracker boxes on a store shelf. Like the tunnel, the street has seen better days.

Every family in every house was having a party of some sort, and every porch and staircase was filled with people. It always seemed like everyone was lighting firecrackers and sparklers and tossing Black Cats and Ladyfingers into the crowd for fun.

A crowd of people had to run a gantlet of fireworks and then funnel themselves into a crowded tunnel, only to wind up in the middle of the biggest crowd anyone could imagine and then have to fight for a spot to watch the show.

It was the show before the show. It was a freak festival.

That's what made the Fourth of July so special—city dwellers and suburbanites, black, white, and Hispanic, rich and poor willing to put up with each other for one day, for one night, for fun. E Pluribus Unum.

—*Tom Papadimoulis*

STREET PARADE: Do-it-yourself celebrations involved the whole neighborhood.

JULY FOURTH OBSERVATION ON ONE LAKEWOOD STREET

I was in the Wayne Avenue July Fourth parades. After I married and had kids, they participated in the parades, too. Kids decorated their bikes, strollers, hot wheels, etc. for the parade, and most wore red, white, and blue clothes. My dad loved playing John Philip Sousa marches on the porch while the parade went by. There were games and refreshments at the armory at the end of the street. I'm not sure if the parade is still going on, but it was a tradition for something like 50 years. Each tree lawn had two flags in the grass. —*Laura Riccardi*

In 1969, Cleveland's summer weather took us by surprise with an unexpected and deadly storm bringing high winds, flooding, and power outages on July Fourth.

BEFORE THE STORM:
Cleveland Mayor Carl Stokes
dedicated Edgewater Park
Pool on July 4, 1969, hours
before a major storm brought
high winds.

SUMMER STORM ON JULY FOURTH

The storm that hit Cleveland suddenly on July 4, 1969, was unforgettable to anyone who experienced it. I was a kid living on East 110th Street at the time. Our cousins lived two doors down and my sister Pam and I, along with our parents, had spent the day with them, stuffing ourselves with the usual hamburgers and hot dogs, baked beans, and macaroni salad and paddling around in their "giant" 4-foot pool playing Marco Polo.

We'd planned to watch fireworks that evening. Instead, the storm swept in out of nowhere, bringing its own brand of fireworks. I remember the sky turning a deep violet and wind swooping in to send loose lawn furniture clattering down the street, while lightning flashed not just downward but horizontally. Our parents barked us into the basement, which was thrilling—to be in your own basement was one thing, but to be in your cousins' basement, which housed their pool table, furniture, and games, was quite another.

We let our mothers carry the fear for us while we played and gallivanted. The big winds passed, leaving us with no electricity but plenty of rain still coming down. We climbed back up the stairs and sat on the front porch watching the rain sheet down, occasional lightning zig-zagging the sky, while our parents talked and laughed around us. Best of all, with the electricity out and a freezer full of popsicles and ice cream bars rapidly melting to goo, we were allowed to eat as many as we could. —*Cindy Washabaugh*

WIND DAMAGE: Summer
storm damage brought the
neighbors out, 1950s.

Summer Eats and Treats

Our summer eating habits were influenced by our location on the shores of Lake Erie, with nearby farms that grew fruits and vegetables. We enjoyed fresh fish caught during fishing trips on Lake Erie, or days spent fishing off a pier. We bought sweet corn and berries from area roadside stands. Other seasonal favorites came right to our homes, thanks to ice cream trucks, the milkman, and all those Charles Chips delivery trucks.

A FARM MEMORY—FROM THE SUBURBS

I grew up in Fairview Village, now Fairview Park. At the time, it was semi-rural, and we lived down the street from a sheep farm. One of my earliest summer memories is when the sheep knocked down the railings of a split-rail fence and there were herds of sheep coming down Wooster Road, filling the street. When I drive through the neighborhood now, I don't recognize anything. The farm is now a huge apartment complex.

When I was growing up, if you wanted peaches or other fruit in the summer, you drove out to Westlake or Bay Village, and you could keep driving down Route 2 to fruit and vegetable stands, farms, and nurseries. —*Howard Schwartz*

Cool Drinks

Remember drinking pop from small bottles at summer picnics? More often than not, those bottles were from Little Tom Bottling Company right here in Cleveland. We also quenched our thirst with lemonade from neighborhood stands run by young entrepreneurs, and learned how to make Kool-Aid with sugar and water. We returned pop bottles to get the deposits so we could roll the money back into even more pop or penny candy. And, in that same era, adults displayed a fondness for locally brewed beers such as Carling.

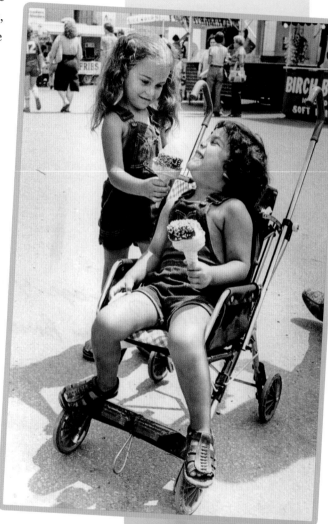

BIG ENOUGH TO SHARE AT THE COUNTY FAIR: Oversized ice cream cones were just one of the midway food choices at the Cuyahoga County Fair, 1981.

Price Check

HERE'S WHAT A NICKEL BOUGHT IN SUMMERS PAST

- A Good Humor Ice Cream Bar during the 1930s

- A cold bottle of Coca-Cola in 1955

- A Hershey chocolate bar in 1965

- Kool-Aid ("A five-cent package makes two full quarts") in the 1960s

GOOD LICK WITH THAT: Ice cream hits the spot in August 1943, as George J. McMonagle (later, Judge McMonagle) poses with St. Joseph orphans during Irish Day at Euclid Beach Park.

A DELICIOUS CYCLE

During the 1950s and 1960s we had to make our own fun during the summer. On Saturday mornings, we would collect empty pop and milk bottles from our neighbors on Rockway Avenue in Lakewood. Then we would head to the corner store, Rockway Deli, to turn in the bottles for money—2 cents for a pop bottle and 5 cents for a milk bottle. We spent the money at the store, buying candy. —*Laura Wirt-Budny*

CHERRY COKES AT SANDERS PHARMACY

On those rare occasions that we had change in our pockets, we would walk up to Sanders Pharmacy in Cleveland Heights and have a cherry Coke from the fountain/bar. —*Sally Slater Wilson*

MAKING YOUR OWN DRINKS

Every day we were over at my best friend's house playing baseball, and it was really hot. We'd go up to the corner deli—Finnegan's, at the corner of Kenilworth and Detroit in Lakewood—and get a packet of Kool-Aid. We would convince my friend's mother to part with a cup of sugar to make it. —*Dave Davis*

RING OF ICE

One of my better memories was hounding the Dairymen's milkman for ice as he was making his deliveries. They were these cool ice rings. This was the early 1960s. —*Paul Negulescu*

Chillin' Out With Ghoulardi

Maybe you remember the advertisements for the Big Ghoulardi drink sold at Manners: "Hey Group, Cool It!" The Big Ghoulardi, introduced in 1963, was promoted as 16 ounces of devilment, made from Ghoulardi's own secret formula. It sold for 35 cents. Here's a memory from someone who drank one.

"During the 1950s and 1960s we had to make our own fun during the summer."

WOULD YOU BELIEVE?
Ghoulardi fans headed to
Manners Big Boy restaurants
to experience this summertime
drink sensation.

A COOL DRINK

For many of us Cleveland baby boomers, Ghoulardi was the Pied Piper of Cool. ("Hey, ova dey! Cool it with the boom-booms!") With his goatee, fright wig, lab coat, and broken Ray-Bans, he was counter-culture before we knew what it was. ("You purple knif!") The hip and wacky midnight movie host had the right combination of anarchy, snark, and tasteless satire to enthrall and inspire his pre-teen demographic. ("Dooor-o-thy?") That also made him eminently marketable. One summer in the mid-'60s, Manners Big Boy touted a new beverage, the Big Ghoulardi. I didn't know what it was, but I knew I had to have one. That wasn't so easy. My family never ate out. Even going to McDonald's was a big deal. Plus, the folks disapproved of my devotion to this dubious role model. I must have been insistent because one evening my older sister grudgingly drove me to the Manners on Lake Shore Boulevard.

This bend of the Boulevard resembled a working-class Vegas with brilliantly lit fast-fooderies and a sprawling pink motel, all in a row. Euclid Beach, the city's rickety amusement park, was down the street. Every evening around closing, the party moved east, beyond Villa Angela and over Euclid Creek to this Lake Shore Babylon. In the summer twilight, neon and dazzling, bulbed signs beckoned the jalopy generation with promises of french fries, frozen custard, and double-decker burgers slathered in special sauce and slaw. High-schoolers, the newly graduated, novice mechanics, and budding beauticians cruised up the strip with the windows down. Turtle-waxed Ramblers, Studebakers, and Plymouths glinted and glided in a slow-motion ballet, with the occasional T-bird or Invicta turning heads. The beats of WIXY Top Sixty tunes throbbed from countless radios.

This Manners was one of the last of the classic drive-in restaurants. Each parking space had a mounted speaker box. My sister pulled in and hit the buzzer. The box barked back. She shouted our order into it, rolled down her window all the way, and we waited. Along the wall, Ghoulardi leered from

DRINKS FOR A DIME

- In 1960, you could buy a cold bottle of Coca-Cola from a vending machine for 10 cents

- In June 1974, a cup of beer cost a dime at Municipal Stadium on Ten Cent Beer Night

SUMMER CHOW: Burger joints, drive-ins, and casual restaurants reigned when it was too hot to cook at home.

ROYAL CASTLE
HAMBURGERS

ROYAL CASTLE
FOOD

Take Home a 6 Pack

spooky blue posters pitching the drink. Blue, as in "Stay sick, turn blue," his signature sendoff. The carhop arrived and hooked the tray onto the driver's door. My sister handed me my cup with the same expression on her face she reserved for those times Mom cooked fish or cauliflower or both. "Disgusting," she sneered, as she reached for her vanilla Coke.

The tall, waxy cup chilled my hand, sending a shudder up my arm. I beheld a milkshake like no other. It was blue, of course, but intense, like robins' eggs, Tiffany gift boxes, or an August sky over Lake Erie. A jolting swirl of orange whipped cream sat plopped on top. The crowning glory was a green maraschino cherry, gleaming like an emerald on a rajah's turban. Blue, orange, green—it was a libation for the eve of the Age of Aquarius.

To be honest, it didn't taste like much. It was thick, and I recall a vaguely citrus bouquet. I wasn't used to shakes and the cold made my teeth ache. I tried not to be let down. I mean, how can the essence of Ghoulardi, the epitome of hipness, be transmuted into a mere flavor?

Any reservations I had, I kept to myself. The simple fact was that I actually drank a Big Ghoulardi. That gave me bragging rights on the playground at Oliver Hazard Perry Elementary School. "A Big Ghoulardi? Sure," I would respond in an off-handed way, pounding a softball into my mitt. "Went to Manners. Had one. It's blue, y'know. It was reeeally gooood." —*Joe Valencic*

Food While We Were Out and About

During trips downtown, the rites of summer often included stops at Hough Bakeries, Higbee's Silver Grille, Halle's Geranium Room, Mills Cafeteria, Stouffer's and other restaurants. In addition, many of the summer events in Northeast Ohio offered the foods we loved. County fairs and festivals were another chance to have corn dogs, elephant ears, cotton candy, and funnel cakes. Other events actually focused on food, including ribs and international fare.

EAT STREET: Al fresco dining at Halle's import bazaar outdoor cafe in 1959.

Stouffer's SHAKER SQUARE

RESTAURANTS

I remember going to restaurants in the summer—the Mark Restaurant at Burke Lakefront Airport, the Howard Johnson's on 55th Street, or Captain Frank's at the end of the Ninth Street Pier. At Howard Johnson's, I loved their clam strips and ice cream. —*Larry Fox*

THE LORAIN INTERNATIONAL FESTIVAL

Summer had truly arrived in the city of Lorain when it was time to drive over to the International Festival. In the years I was growing up, it was held in a sort of weeded-over parking lot of the May Company, which was kind of off the beaten path behind a little shopping center. But once every summer, it was transformed.

The main attraction was the food. Lorain is a real melting pot of cultures and flavors, and most Lorainites are super proud of this.

There were two huge rows of makeshift stands with little portable kitchens behind them. The smoke, the sizzle, and the aromas rising up just made you ravenous and eager to pick a line to get into.

Old ladies from local churches—Puerto Rican, Polish, Greek, Slovenian, and more—would have done some prep work beforehand. There were big vats of cabbage and noodles, the buttery side dish that was perfect to get started with in a little paper square. I'd dig into it with gusto, using a plastic fork that was going to snap if I wasn't careful. We'd keep walking to find the next dish, eating, saying hello to friends from school, trying not to drop any of the gyro or fried rice.

I was never more proud to be Hungarian than when I'd notice the line was like three times longer than at the other booths. Chicken paprikash was the draw, that velvety, sour-creamy concoction that takes you to the prototypical Eastern European grandmother's kitchen of the mind.

The other standouts in my mind were the pasteles and rice and beans from the Puerto Rican booths: succulent, salty, with huge chunks of pork throughout, washed down with some orange pop from the beverage booth.

And as kids, it was always fun gawking at the "International Princesses," teenage girls dressed up in peasant garb. Big, starchy skirts always played a part for some reason, and sashes, red and green ribbons, and African head wraps worn with a tiara, looking so cool, ready to jump on stage for some Irish dance at the drop of a hat. Polka music was ever-present, too, as was the thought: "Oh my God, it's almost the end of June! Summer is slipping away from me!" Boy, was it ever. —*Tara York Ellis Fitzpatrick*

Don't Heat Up the Kitchen

If you didn't want to cook at home, or just wanted to grab something cool, here's what it cost to go out:

- 1963: A Big Ghoulardi milkshake at Manners Big Boy was 35 cents
- 1965: A McDonald's milkshake cost 22 cents
- 1965: French fries or a hamburger cost 15 cents at McDonald's; a McDouble Cheeseburger was 38 cents
- 1968: The Friday night fried clam dinners at Howard Johnson's were $1.49
- 1968: A Big Mac at McDonald's was 49 cents

SMOKE GOT IN YOUR EYES: Coventry Street Fair food, 1984.

MADE IN THE SHADE: Picnicking on the lawn before a concert at Blossom Music Center.

Picnic-Baskers

Picnics were more than meals. They were summertime social events. We basked in the warmth of get-togethers, and reveled in the flavors and fun that families and friends brought to picnics. We cooked on grills in the city parks to escape our hot kitchens. We transported foods like fried chicken, ambrosia salad, pickled eggs, stuffed cabbage, and deep-dish peach pies to family reunions.

There's no doubt that food connects us to our families, our neighborhood, and our own childhood. At picnics, we not only got together with relatives, we also enjoyed the food traditions of our family cultures and various ethnic heritages.

TONIGHT'S DINNER OPTIONS: A RESTAURANT OR A TAKE-OUT ORDER PICNIC?

Our parents both worked full-time, which created our summer dinner ritual. Instead of saying, "What should we have for dinner?" they would ask, "Where should we go for dinner tonight?" The restaurants were air-conditioned, which was something we didn't have at home. Most often our choice was Kenny King's, where you could pick a toy out of the treasure chest after dinner. Other favorites were Manners and Still's Diner, both on Detroit Avenue in Lakewood.

We also had picnics in the valley (Rocky River Reservation Metropark) or at Lakewood Park. My mom's idea of a picnic was Kenny King's takeout—a bucket of chicken with side dishes that fit perfectly into her picnic basket, along with a table cloth. —*Laurie Ghetia-Orr*

COTTAGE COOK-OUTS

We would rent a cottage with friends along the west side of Cleveland on Lake Erie. We would have a pig roast with corn on the cob and shoot skeet over the lake. —*Sally Slater Wilson*

RED, WHITE, AND BLUE FOOD ON JULY 4TH

We were having a family celebration on July Fourth when our kids were in elementary school. My nieces, nephews, and some of the neighbor children were in the backyard playing with July Fourth red, white, and blue cupcakes I had made.

MINDING OUR MANNERS: You could dine in the privacy of your own car at the Manners Drive-In Restaurant at 17655 Lake Shore Boulevard.

In fact, they were throwing them. A neighbor called the police because she didn't know what they were doing crawling around on their hands and knees in my backyard. The police came to the back door and said, "What's going on here? We've had a complaint." I apologized and asked if we were too loud. He said, no, there are people in the bushes and your neighbors don't know what's going on.

It was the kids in the bushes, looking for the cupcakes. I asked the policeman if he wanted a cupcake. He said no, he was on duty, but he was laughing. —*Joann Rae Macias*

FOOD ON THE FARM IN AVON

My grandmother was an amazing baker because her mother-in-law had been an apprentice baker in Hungary. Every weekend in the summer we would drive out to her farm in Avon, before the highway, and take old Lake Road all the way. She had a 60-plus acre farm on a cul-de-sac dirt road. She'd be baking about 10 cakes or pies at a time, running around, chasing all the animals—which she had named—with a broom in her hand. And I particularly remember her favorite cow, Patricia, who was always escaping and going to the neighbors' homes. And one day it came time to butcher Patricia. The huge dining room table sat about 24 people, and she made some kind of fabulous beef roast meal with spaetzle and vegetables from the garden, and all we could think about was Patricia.

After dinner we'd have bonfires outside. —*Larry Fox*

HOLIDAY FAMILY PICNICS

We had lot of family picnics with cousins, aunts, uncles, and grandparents. You could always count on a big party for Memorial Day, the 4th of July, and Labor Day. There always seemed to be family reunions every summer, also. —*Noreen Hone*

GREAT FOOD

We had a really large family. Everybody was an Eastern European immigrant. We had our family reunion picnic at Euclid Beach, and then later we had it at Geauga Lake. There would be a couple hundred people. We had sack races, crab walks, relays . . . I remember all the fathers were always sitting in those woven lounge chairs that would fold up. My father was a pretty big guy, and if those chairs were a little bit worn he'd go through them. He weighed about 275 pounds and those things were made for someone like

HOT DOG NUMBERS

Mention summer memories of Euclid Beach Park or Cleveland Municipal Stadium and chances are somebody will mention eating great hot dogs. That's because according the National Hot Dog and Sausage Council, hot dog season runs from Memorial Day to Labor Day, a time during which Americans typically polish off 7 billion hot dogs. On July Fourth alone, the nation puts away 150 million hot dogs. The Council says that's enough hot dogs to span the distance from Washington, D.C. to Los Angeles—five times!

GRILL TALK: Higbee's customers could check out this barbecue grill while they were shopping downtown.

MESSAGE IN A BOTTLE: Carling's summertime promotions tapped into our preferences for locally made Carling Black Label beer. The Cleveland plant closed in 1971.

FOOD AND MUSIC: At this 1938 picnic, Joe Valencic entertains on his Cleveland-made Mervar accordion.

my mother, who weighed 98 pounds. All the photos show the guys in their lounge chairs, and the wives preparing meals.

We had great, great food. A lot of the family was Hungarian, so we would have stuffed peppers. There would be paprikash. One guy was a caterer, so he did all kinds of great sandwiches. I mean, you got stuffed! Every good food group. There were deli trays and desserts, and then you'd go get cotton candy at the amusement park. If you were a little kid, you walked in there weighting 72 pounds and you walked out weighing 78 pounds. Our picnic was in a little grassy area right underneath where the rocket ships were—the Rocket Ride at Euclid Beach. —*Steve Presser*

Other fond memories include company picnics, lodge picnics, and large get-togethers of friends.

FOOD WITH FRIENDS

Summer reminds me of Huntington Beach picnics with my friends. One year, we decided to gather some friends for a picnic. It evolved into break-fast early in the morning and lasted the entire day. This picnic among our friends became an annual event for a number of years and the number attending it grew each year. It was great to get together with everyone outside of the bars. —*Nancy Reese*

FARMS FOR FUN

Beer gardens had been a summer tradition among Cleveland's nationality groups since the late 1800s. With the onset of Prohibition, some farmers hosted Sunday picnics on their outlying properties where guests could enjoy music for dancing, food, lawn bowling, horseshoes, and homemade wine and moonshine. My parents lived in the St. Clair-Superior neighborhood. They would meet their friends after church at the Oblak Furniture store and ride in the moving van to farm dances in distant Euclid, Wickliffe or North Olmsted.

When beer, wine, and liquor were legal again, nationality fraternal societies and lodges bought farms (some casualties of the Great Depression) and built pavilions with dance floors and kitchens. These summer getaways became warm-weather alter-natives to nationality halls in the city with dances, fund-raisers, festivals, sports, and beauty contests. A few, such as German Central Farm in Parma and S. N. P. J. (Slovene National Benefit Society) Recreation Grounds in Kirtland, are still active today. —*Joe Valencic*

Getting in Your Licks: Cool Ice Cream Memories

Northeast Ohio offered many opportunities to enjoy cold treats—ice cream trucks, soda fountains, ice cream parlors, and refreshment stands. Sometimes an ice cream store was the destination, but in other cases, it was a refreshing stop along the way to someplace else. To this day, many adults have a Pavlovian response to hearing popular ice cream truck songs like "Pop Goes the Weasel" and "Turkey in the Straw," that always seemed to sound like they were being played on a toy piano. Something about those songs makes us crave Creamsicles, Fudgsicles, and Popsicles.

Depending on the era when you grew up, you had lots of ice cream choices. In the Fifties, most communities offered drug store soda fountains and ice cream shops where you could order an ice cream soda or a sundae. Downtown shoppers were wowed by Boukair's, with its glitzy interior and whimsically named sundaes, and made special trips to the Frosty Bar in Higbee's basement to get a Frosty Malt served, sans spoon, in a tall glass. In the '60s, your mother might have sent you over to the closest Lawson's store on your bike to pick up a half-gallon of Lawson's Ice Milk, or Franklin's Ice Cream for some ice cream cups with wooden spoons. In Berea, Isaly's was popular in the late '50s and early '60s. In the late '50s, Dairy Queen made its mark on Cleveland with ice cream cones that had signature curlicues on top.

COOL CARTS: Ewing Ice Cream was sold from carts in Rocky River in the 1950s.

THE QUEEN OF EXPERIENCES

I remember going to Dairy Queen. The amazing thing is that when we went there, the largest ice cream cone cost 25 cents. Even though I was a fairly little person, I would get the twenty-five-cent ice cream cone, which was huge. Your biggest challenge was to keep it from dripping all over you.

I have another ice cream memory, too. Sometimes my grandmother would take us out to somewhere east that they called The Farm, and people would bring a lot of food. They had sausage and whiskey and then polka. As my grandmother was driving us out there, somewhere around Cleveland, she got us ice cream and it did start to melt. My brother had a chocolate cone and didn't know what to do with it because it was melting so he just held it out the window. My grandmother had a white car, and as we were driving it got chocolate ice cream all over the side. The farm we were driving to might have been owned by a Slovenian organization. It wasn't a working farm; it was more like a park. —*Maribeth Katt*

CONE RANGERS: In 1959, the combination of a 1-cent sale and a hot day brought a neighborhood crowd to the Dairy Queen at West 58th and Memphis.

BIG DIPPERS: A local favorite ice cream spot was Boukair's at Playhouse Square downtown.

CLEVELAND HEIGHTS ICE CREAM TRUCK

When I think of summer when I was a young child, the very first image that pops into my brain is sitting on the sidewalk stoop, sometimes right on the street curb, waiting anxiously for the faint and familiar sound of Uncle Marty's Ice Cream Truck. As the sound of his musical bells approached, I would start yelling to my mother, "Mommy, it's Unca-Mawdy, Unca-Mawdy's coming." My mother would bring me my dime and I was a happy camper. Uncle Marty was a typically sweet old guy who loved kids, and his little white truck—that now looks like a truck you would see in a cartoon—delighted me more than anything. His Popsicles came in the shape of a Creamsicle. There were two wrapped in a white paper wrapper. I always got one and shared the other with my mom or a neighbor kid. Cherry was my favorite and they had a flavor and smell that I've searched to find for 50 years. There is no cherry flavor like Uncle Marty's cherry Popsicle. We lived at Glenmont and Superior in Cleveland Heights, right across from Forest Hill Park. Uncle Marty is my favorite childhood memory. —*Julie Matthews*

ICONIC ICE CREAM CONE IN NORTH COLLINWOOD

I remember what we called the "upside down ice cream cone." It was located in the North Collinwood area on Lakeshore Boulevard. What I really recall is not when it was an ice cream parlor. For years during the Christmas season, they sold live Christmas trees. My family went there for years to buy our tree. I wish I had taken photos of it before it was torn down. —*John Laws*

GOOD MEMORIES OF GOOD HUMOR IN SHAKER HEIGHTS

I grew up in Shaker Heights and remember most fondly the Good Humor truck coming down our street, Ingleside Road, maybe every day. All the neighborhood kids would gather around. It was a real treat. —*Jackie Finn*

NAME GAME: Creatively named sundaes were part of the package at Boukair's.

FAIRVIEW ICE CREAM FANS

I remember Weber's Ice Cream at West 220th Street and Lorain. That was terrific. I used to go there all the time. There was also a Franklin's Ice Cream that was near the high school, and was a big hang-out for the high school kids. But Weber's had the greatest soft serve ice cream, and they were one of the first to have that hard chocolate dip. —*Howard Schwartz*

BOSTON COOLERS IN ROCKY RIVER

A standard on a hot summer day was Boston Coolers, made with root beer and ice cream. As a kid, I always wanted Dairy Queen, and our parents always said no. My parents always took us to Weber's on Hilliard Road in Rocky River, and we got the real stuff. Weber's still exists, now up on Lorain. —*Dave Davis*

ICE CREAM MEMORIES IN LAKEWOOD

We remember eating ice cream at Malley's and other places. It was fun to stop in the drug stores like Winton Drug and Webb Drug and get a drink at the soda fountain. —*Karl and Laura Riccardi*

ICE CREAM CONES IN GEAUGA LAKE

An ideal summer day was getting up early, taking a hike around the wooded area near our cottage, then going down to the residents' swimming area at Geauga Lake. We'd enjoy that for a couple of hours, and then go across the street to a delicatessen/general store called Lyons that had wonderful ice cream cones, hotdogs, and sandwiches for lunch. Then we'd head back to the cottage for a quick nap and in the late afternoon, head over to Geauga Lake Amusement Park to spend the early evening riding all the rides.
—*Dennis Gaughan*

One ice cream fan recalls some favorite ice cream experiences more than 70 years ago at a soda fountain, in a drug store that opened in 1909.

SUNDAES IN HUDSON

When I was 12, I went to Girl Scout Camp at Camp Ledgewood in Peninsula. They would take us over to Hudson, to Saywell's Pharmacy, for hot fudge sundaes. The pharmacy closed around 2005. It had been in business more than 90 years. —*Nancy Sorgi*

BUY THE HALF GALLON:
Everybody had a favorite ice cream flavor.

DID YOU KNOW?

In 1924, the ice cream cone rolling machine was patented by Clevelander Carl R. Taylor, making it possible to produce more ice cream cones and do it faster.

IN THE NIFTY '50S AND '60s: Beaches, camps, amusement parks, community events, and neighborhoods were filled with summer fun.

WHAT GOES AROUND COMES AROUND

Recapturing Summers Past

I f you're nostalgic about Euclid Beach, you'll want to know that in some cases, what went around has come around. This is especially true if you're talking about favorite rides, Laughing Sal and even some of the food.

THE HUMPHREY POPCORN, POPCORN BALLS AND CANDY KISSES YOU LOVED AT EUCLID BEACH

Fans of Euclid Beach will be delighted to know they can find Humphrey Kisses and Humphrey Popcorn, including the popcorn balls, in many area grocery stores. On the Humphrey Company website, you can also buy ornaments (Laughing Sal, The Bug, Rock-O-Plane, Great American Racing Derby and Laff in the Dark) and a CD recorded live at Euclid Beach featuring waltzes played on the Gavioli Band organ.

THE RACING DERBY RIDES AGAIN

It's now named Cedar Downs Racing Derby, but it's the same Great American Racing Derby classic carousel you fell in love with at Euclid Beach. It now draws crowds at Cedar Point in Sandusky, and is one of only two racing carousels in the country. In 2013, it was featured in *USA Today* in "10 Great Places: These Carousels are Worth Your Whirl." The opinion? The 1920s carousel was singled out both for its speed (15 miles per hour) and for the fact that the horses slide forward and backward in their rows, creating the illusion of a race.

FLAVOR OF EUCLID BEACH: Savor the nostalgic flavors of popcorn and candy kisses.

HUMPHREY POPCORN CO.
20810 Miles Parkway
Warrensville Hts., OH 44128
216-662-6629
www.humphreycompany.com

WILLIAM KLESS STUDIO
wkstudio@roadrunner.com

THE EUCLID BEACH ROCKET CAR
Ron Heitman, Captain
www.therocketcar.com
216-382-1616

A RACING DERBY MEMORY

Euclid Beach always had the Racing Derby carousel, where the four horses were lined up in a row and you never knew which of the four horses was going to win. It was in a large pavilion area that rotated, and the horses would move forward and backward. —*Dennis Gaughan*

VISIONS OF EUCLID BEACH

Local artist William Kless preserves the spirit of the era with his illustrations of Euclid Beach, including illustrations of the entrance gate, Laughing Sal, and a poster with numerous Euclid Beach attractions. "The thing about Euclid Beach," he says, "was that they had Nickel Days and School Days. There were a lot of people who didn't have much money and didn't want to spend what little they had. I talk with a lot of people who only got there on Nickel Days and when they got tickets for School Days—on freebie and discount days."

"The Flying Turns, The Thriller, the Rocket Ships, and the dance hall, Flying Scooters, Kiddie Land, the ice cream, popcorn balls, and taffy are probably the things that almost everybody remembers." Kless adds, "I can't paint all your memories, but I can stimulate them."

THE BEAUTY OF EUCLID BEACH

Even at a young age, I recognized the beauty of Euclid Beach being on the lake, and the Ballroom. The Ballroom wasn't being used by the time we went there, but it was still there and you could see the beautiful glass windows that looked right over the lake. I loved the entrance because, in my recollection, as soon as you walked in you saw the silver Rocket Ships going around and also another ride, the Butterflies, but they were called something else. They were my kind of thing. They weren't scary rides, they just went around the big pillar they were attached to. I think that entrance has to be one of the most elegant entrances to an amusement park anywhere. —*Maribeth Katt*

YOUR MEMORIES RIDE AGAIN WITH EUCLID BEACH ROCKET CARS

Two Euclid Beach Rocket Cars are available for company picnics, parades, weddings, reunions, block parties and more, through Ron Heitman, Captain of the Euclid Beach Rocket Car. His slogan: "Your entertainment is our rocket science."

Each year, the St. Patrick's Day Parade launches the season for the Euclid Beach Rocket Car, and public events are halted when the winter weather heads in, although Heitman says he does some Christmas events.

He tells his Rocket Car story: "We went to Euclid Beach as children, and went there right up until the end. In 1978, I was driving up a side street off East 152nd Street and spotted the rocket sitting on the ground in a guy's back yard. That same afternoon, I was preparing an Olds Toronado to drive in a demolition derby the following week, and I was looking at the drive train and thought, *Wow, I think I could make that work in the rocket.* I measured it out, went back down there, and introduced myself to the guy. He had bought it in 1969 for his kids to play in, but they grew up and moved away, and now he had 'Shamu' in the backyard. I bought the rocket, and three-and-a-half months later, we had a car."

EUCLID BEACH ENVY

I completely missed Euclid Beach Amusement Park. By 1974, when I arrived in Cleveland, it was closed. I figured I'd have to be content with East Coast Custard and Euclid Beach popcorn balls. I didn't know about the Rocket Car. One very hot summer Sunday in the mid-1980s, I was walking down Lee Road in Cleveland Heights. The street was quiet, and there was very little traffic. Suddenly, a huge, silver, cigar-shaped, finned thing blaring calliope music zoomed past and disappeared down a side street. I thought maybe I was having a heat-stroke hallucination, but I found out that I'd seen a Euclid Beach rocket car, beautifully restored for road travel by Ron Heitman. I finally got a rocket car ride at the Cedar Fairmount arts festival. It was awesome, but I was disappointed we had to stop for red lights. —*Meredith Holmes*

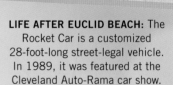

LIFE AFTER EUCLID BEACH: The Rocket Car is a customized 28-foot-long street-legal vehicle. In 1989, it was featured at the Cleveland Auto-Rama car show.

JOE TOMARO AND JOHN FRATO
EuclidBeachBoys@aol.com
440-460-0565
www.euclidbeachpark.com

LAUGHING SAL, THE ROCKET SHIP CAR, THE THRILLER CAR AND PARK MEMORABILIA

The Euclid Beach Boys (Joe Tomaro and John Frato) can help you recapture your Euclid Beach memories for special events with the Rocket Ship Car, the Thriller Car and Laughing Sal, from May 1 through November 1. Their motto is "Preserving Cleveland's Amusement History, One Piece at a Time." Joe Tomaro says, "People here so appreciate things because it was such a big part of their lives when they were growing up. They didn't have a lot of money to spend, so they were able to go the park for a few cents, ride a ride or two, and watch people. They entertained themselves and forgot about the wars that were going on and the Depression and everything else. It was something that was affordable. That's why this park had such a special place in the history of Cleveland amusement."

Tomaro adds, "The Rocket Ships and The Thriller—along with the Flying Turns—were among the most popular rides in the park. Laughing Sal was the icon of the park. She is still extremely popular. I think she will be for generations to come. She is one of the original four papier-mache Sals that are left. We're pretty protective of her. She ran 18 hours a day when the park was operating. Some of her mechanics are pretty rigid, but the papier-mache part, the cosmetic part, is critical.

"We have the Rocket Ship Car—the Euclid Beach ride was called The Rocket Ships—and one of The Thriller cars that's motorized. We do traveling displays and are currently in the process of opening up one of our storage areas to the public so they can view some of what we have—over 25,000 square feet of park memorabilia in storage. It's coming in 2014. We also have some things from Geauga Lake and Chippewa Lake. This younger generation remembers Geauga Lake, and Chippewa Lake goes back to 1978. Prior to Geauga Lake closing, we accumulated a lot of the older things that were stored on the property."

THE EUCLID BEACH CAROUSEL MAKES A COMEBACK

In 2013, the Western Reserve Historical Society (WRHS) and the Cleveland Carousel Society began their public fundraising project to raise the remaining funds needed to reassemble and restore the Euclid Beach Park Carousel at the Glass Pavilion of the WRHS. The Carousel had approximately a 60-year run at Euclid Beach Park and will once again be back in action.

RELIVE THE TASTE: HIGBEE'S FROSTY MALT AND PREMIUM CUSTARD À LA EUCLID BEACH FROZEN WHIP

Ice cream-lovers can get in their licks with taste memories of the cool Frosty Malts sold in tall glasses (without spoons, you'll recall) in the basement of Higbee's downtown, and the style of satisfyingly rich premium custard that won so many loyal fans at Euclid Beach. All it takes is a visit to Weber's Premium Custard and Ice Cream in Fairview Park. It's open seasonally, from April through October.

WESTERN RESERVE HISTORICAL SOCIETY

10825 East Boulevard
Cleveland, OH 44106
216-721-5722
www.clevelandcarousel.org
www.wrhs.org

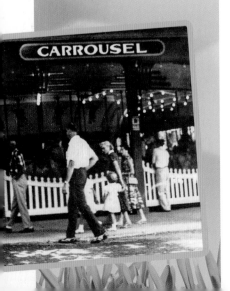

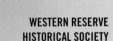

GIVE IT A WHIRL: "The Humphreys gave rides unique spellings. The Carousel was originally 'Carousal,' then it became 'Carrousel.' For its new life, it will have the conventional spelling," says John Frato, executive board secretary of Cleveland's Euclid Beach Park Carousel Society.

Regarding the taste of Euclid Beach Frozen Whip, owner David Ford says, "We make premium custard, not frozen custard. The vanilla premium custard is the same that was made at Euclid Beach. It did not have egg yolks in it. Egg yolks were the first cheapening of the mix, when people took out cream and put in egg fat, which was only one-seventh the cost of cream."

And for the special flavor of the Frosty Malts, Ford credits the ice cream machines as well as the recipe. "This is the last pair of the original ice cream machines designed by the Vogt Brothers out of Louisville in 1879. The pair was made after the paradigm for ice-cream making was changed, made by special request for Mr. Weber. The new paradigm was 10 quarts of mix in, 20 quarts of ice cream out, which is still the standard today. These machines are 10 quarts in, 14 quarts out." He says the frosted malts were originally intended to be sold in ice cream cones in Higbee's basement. However, the soft-serve ice cream wouldn't sit on cones. Instead, it was served in old soda fountain glasses. "It was a huge success. People couldn't walk out with the glass, so they wandered around, shopped, and bought."

RECALLING HOUGH BAKERIES

You can recapture some of your Hough Bakeries favorites, including cakes, from Archie's Lakeshore Bakery. The shop was started by the former head baker at the catering department of Hough Bakeries, Archie Garner, and brings a blast from Hough's past into the present.

RECAPTURE THE CAR CULTURE AT A DRIVE-IN THEATER

The number of drive-in movie theaters may be dwindling nationally, with only about 360 still operating, but you can still enjoy a movie in your own car. Built in 1965, the family-owned Aut-O-Rama Twin Drive-In, North Ridgeville, is now operated by a third generation of the Sherman family. In 1972, it became the Twin Drive-in, with movie-goers having their choice of features. Its regular season is from the beginning of April through the end of September.

REVISIT MEMPHIS KIDDIE PARK

It opened in May, 1952 with 10 rides. Today, the kiddie park offers 11 rides, many of which you might remember from your childhood. Among them, says owner/president Russell Winter, are the merry-go-round, Ferris wheel, boat, and roller coaster rides, although most have been restored and have had parts replaced.

WEBER'S PREMIUM CUSTARD AND ICE CREAM
David Ford
20230 Lorain Road
Fairview Park, OH 44126
440-331-0004

ARCHIE'S LAKESHORE BAKERY
14906 Lake Shore Boulevard
Cleveland
216-481-4188

AUT-O-RAMA TWIN DRIVE-IN
33395 Lorain Road
N. Ridgeville, OH 44039
440-327-9595
www.autoramdrivein.com

MEMPHIS KIDDIE PARK
10340 Memphis Ave.
Brooklyn, OH 44144
216-941-5995
www.memphiskiddiepark.com

PHOTO CREDITS

ACKNOWLEDGMENTS

Once again I find myself owing heaps of gratitude to Stephen Bellamy for his editorial vision, to Laurie Ghetia-Orr for her photo and memory collecting ability, and to editor Rob Lucas of Gray & Company, whose unerring sense of nostalgia is exceeded only by his editing talent.

I also thank those who offered expertise, shared their enthusiasm, pointed me in the right direction, and provided photos and memorabilia to enrich this collection of memories. Each of them has contributed to our collective memory of Cleveland summers past: Carol Evans Abel; Sheila Bellamy; Bunny Breslin; Bill Chase, The Cleveland Public Library; Ken Brady, The Paper Chasers ; Wendy Brewer, Joseph-Beth Booksellers; Kathleen Cerveny; Gary Cardot Photography; Cecilia Dolgan; James W. Dowd; The Euclid Beach Boys, John Frato and Joe Tomaro; Tommy Fello; Patricia M. Fernberg; Patrick Flynn; Larry Fox; Diane Francis; George Ghetia; Joe Gunderman; Deborah M. Hefling, archivist, The Musical Arts Association; Alan and Joan Hitchcox; Andria Hoy, Archives Assistant, The Cleveland Orchestra; Jeff Iula; Bonnie Jacobson; Laurie Kincer, Cuyahoga County Public Library; William Kless Studio; Nicole Loughman; John Lawn; Russ Lowe; Tony Macias; Lynette Macias; the McLaughlin Family; Jane Mason, Western Reserve Historical Society; Glen Nekvasil; Jennifer K. Nieves, Archivist, Dittrick Medical History Center, CWRU; Kara Hamley O'Donnell, City Planner/Historic Preservation Planner/Storefront Program Coordinator, City of Cleveland Heights Department of Planning and Development; Laurie Ghetia-Orr; Ware Petznick, Ph.D., Shaker Historical Society; Wendy Pittenger, Penitentiary Glen Nature Center; George Popovich; Steve Presser, Big Fun; Nancy Reese; Stephanie Clements, Shaker Historical Society; Kim St. John-Stevenson; Niki Sherman; Eric J. Silverman of the Cleveland Heights High School Alumni Foundation; Nancy Hudson Snell; Mercy Sorgi and Nancy Sorgi, The American Fireworks Company; Joe Valencic; Laura Whalen, Interlibrary Loan Assistant, Allen Medical Library, CWRU; and Sally Slater Wilson.

The following folks also shared a piece of their pasts with summertime memories: Carol Evans Abel; Deanna R. Adams; Marge Adler; Sam Bell; John Stark Bellamy II; Stephen Bellamy; Bunny Breslin; Laura Wirt-Budny; Istvan Burgyan; Kathleen Cerveny; Dave Davis; Suzanne DeGaetano; Lisa Gollwitzer Dixon; Pat Fernberg; Jackie Finn; Tara York Ellis Fitzpatrick; Patrick Flynn; David Ford; Larry Fox; John Frato; Dennis Gaughan; Stephanie Gautam; George Ghetia; Joe Gunderman; Ron Heitman; Alan Hitchcox; Emily Hitchcox; Joanie Hitchcox; Meredith Holmes; Noreen Hone; Steve Horniak; Christine Howey; Renee Hanna Irvin; Bonnie Jacobson; Debbie Jancsurak; Joe Jancsurak; Maribeth Katt; William Kless; Donna "Dahmia" Komidar; Mark Krieger; Carol Lally; John Laws; Nicole Loughman; Joann Rae Macias; Lynette Macias; Tony Macias; Christy Callaghan McLaughlin; Lynne McLaughlin; Julie Matthews; Leo Michitsch; Barbara Mongelluzzi; Terry Morgan; Paul Negulescu; Peggy King-Neumann; Erin O'Brien; Toni Oliverio; Laurie Ghetia-Orr; Molly Orr; Nikole Ortiz; Tom Papadimoulis; Steve Presser; George Popovich; Nancy Reese; Mark Rhoades; Laura Riccardi; Karl Riccardi; Linda Goodman Robiner; Chuck "Big Chuck" Schodowski; Howard Schwartz; Deb Sherman; Nancy Hudson Snell; Mercy Sorgi; Nancy Sorgi; Peggy Spaeth; Fred Taub; Joe Tomaro; Maria Trivisonno; Joe Valencic; Dave Vogt; Walt Wagner; Cindy Washabaugh; Rhea Wightman; Sally Slater Wilson; Russell Winter and Helen Wirt.

More Cleveland Memories . . .

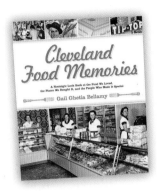

Cleveland Food Memories
by Gail Ghetia Bellamy

Remember when food was local? Cleveland companies made it, and local people sold it and ran the restaurants where we ate it. Now, take a delicious trip into the past.

Food makes powerful memories. Mention Hough Bakery and see how quickly we Clevelanders start to drool over just the thought of those long-lost white cakes. How about a Frosty in the Higbee's basement. Popcorn balls at Euclid Beach. Burgers at Manners or Mawby's. Entertainment-filled nights at Alpine Village. Mustard at old Municipal Stadium . . . and so much more.

Paperback / 112 pages / 209 photos

Cleveland Christmas Memories
by Gail Ghetia Bellamy

What made Christmas extra-special to a Cleveland kid? Come relive some of your fondest moments . . .

Seeing Mr. Jingeling (the keeper of Santa's keys) on TV or in person at Halle's. Gazing at the giant Sterling-Lindner tree. Ice skating on Public Square. The brilliant holiday lighting display at GE's Nela Park . . .

Join in as dozens of Northeast Ohioans share their personal stories of Christmas past; includes recollections of people who made Christmas happen, too: former Santas, retail window dressers, entertainers, and of course parents.

Paperback / 126 pages / 234 photos

Cleveland Amusement Park Memories
by David and Diane Francis

Northeast Ohioans who grew up visiting amusement parks in the 1940s through 1970s will cherish these memories of Euclid Beach Park, Luna Park, Geauga Lake Park, Puritas Springs Park, White City, Memphis Kiddie Park, Geneva-on-the-Lake, and others.

Each park had its own personality, its own alluring smells and sounds. At Euclid Beach it was the stately sycamores and the unforgettable odor of the lake and of damp earth beneath the pier. At Puritas Springs, the odor of warm oil on the chain of the Cyclone coaster. The chatter of Monkey Island at Luna Park, the sharp reports of the Shooting Gallery at Geauga Lake.

Paperback / 128 pages / 192 photos

Cleveland Rock & Roll Memories
by Carlo Wolff

Clevelanders who grew up with Rock and Roll in the 1960s, '70s, and '80s remember a golden age, with clubs like the Agora, trendsetting radio stations WIXY 1260 and WMMS, Coffee Break Concerts, The World Series of Rock. Includes first-person stories by fans, musicians, DJs, reporters, club owners, and more, with rare photos and memorabilia.

Paperback / 136 pages / 203 photos

More information and samples at: **www.grayco.com**